MATHEMATICS WORKSHOP

PROBLEM SOLVING 2

REVISED EDITION

GLOBE FEARON EDUCATIONAL PUBLISHER
Upper Saddle River, New Jersey
www.globefearon.com

Consultant:
Dr. Alan Barson
Director, Chapter 1 Secondary Mathematics Program
City of Philadelphia
Philadelphia, Pennsylvania

Art and Design Credits:
Illustrations: Judy Love
Cover design: Marjory Dressler

Developed and produced for Globe Fearon by **Publicom, Inc.**

Printed in the United States of America

2 3 4 5 6 7 8 9 10 03 02 01 00

ISBN: 0-130-23358-7 (Student Edition)
ISBN: 0-130-23366-8 (Annotated Teacher's Edition)

GLOBE FEARON EDUCATIONAL PUBLISHER
Upper Saddle River, New Jersey
www.globefearon.com

Contents

Introductory Lesson

Aim: To learn how lessons are organized in this book, and to start thinking about word problems

What You Need to Know

The lessons in *Mathematics Workshop: Problem Solving 2* have the same organization as the lessons in Book 1. If you have not done *Problem Solving 1,* check with your teacher to make sure you are in the right book.

Unit 1 in Book 2 is a review of Book 1. In Unit 1, you will review the five problem solving steps. In Units 2 and 3, you will practice the strategies learned in Book 1 for solving different types of problems. You will also learn some new strategies. In Unit 4, you will see just how important it is in everyday life to be able to solve problems.

As in Book 1, each lesson begins with an "Aim," telling you what you will learn in the lesson. This is followed by three major sections: "What You Need to Know," "Think About It," and "Practice."

Book 1 gave me the right key.

Name three major ideas that this Introductory Lesson says you "need to know."

_____

_____

_____

You probably remember that the "Think About It" section always starts with a question. Like the question above, it is about something you read in the "What You Need to Know" section.

After the question, there are one or two Examples. The Examples are word problems. They show how to apply the new information. Also, they are similar to the Practice problems you will be doing in the third section of the lesson.

How many units are in this book?

Answer: *There are 4 units.*

The map shows the route Brad takes when he walks from his home to school each morning. How far does Brad walk to school?

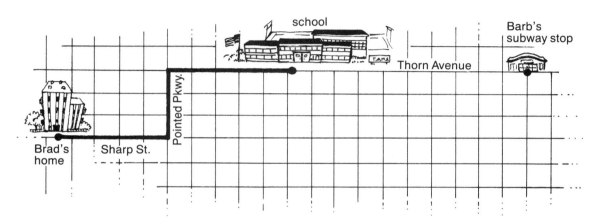

Step 1 (Read, reread, and reword): *How many blocks from school does Brad live?*

Step 2 (Find the needed facts): *Blocks on Sharp Street: 4.5; blocks on Pointed Parkway: 3; blocks on Thorn Avenue: 5.25*

Step 3 (Plan what to do): *Add (blocks on Sharp + blocks on Pointed + blocks on Thorn = total number of blocks)*
   Sometimes, Step 3 also includes making an estimate: 5 + 3 + 5 = 13.

Step 4 (Carry out the plan):
$$\begin{array}{r} 4.50 \\ 3.00 \\ + 5.25 \\ \hline 12.75 \end{array}$$
Answer:
12.75 blocks

Step 5 (Check the answer): *Is answer reasonable? Yes. Does computation check? Yes.* (In this case, you would add "backward": 5.25 + 3.00 + 4.50 = 12.75.)

Both Examples apply what you are learning to a specific situation. Example B also gives you a brief review of the steps you learned in Book 1.

   Remember from Book 1, after the Examples there is a paragraph. Like the one above, the paragraph says something more about the Examples.

Practice

The third section in each lesson is "Practice." This is where you show how well you have understood the lesson. If you have trouble with the problems in this section, study the first two sections again.

1. What does the first unit in Book 2 do? _____

   _____

2. After "Aim," what is the first section in each lesson called?

   _____

3. In which section of the lesson are the Examples found?

   _____

4. Show how you would **estimate** an answer to the following computations.

   a. 110×9: _____ × _____ = _____

   b. $198 \div 11$: _____ ÷ _____ = _____

5. Read this word problem. Use the map in Example B to answer the questions that follow.

   Barb rides the subway between school and home twice a day. How far does she ride the subway each day?

   a. What fact is needed from the map? _____

   b. In this word problem, would a final answer of 3 blocks make sense? Why or why not?

   _____

   _____

As in Book 1, there is a Unit Review at the end of each unit in Book 2. Look at the Unit 1 Review on pages 14–16 to remind yourself about the types of questions that appear in a Unit Review.

The following sections are found at the end of the book:

- Additional Practice items for each lesson (pages 83–115)
- Whole-Book Review (pages 116–119)
- Appendix (pages 120–122)

Look at each of these sections. They should all seem familiar. They are similar to the sections at the end of *Problem Solving 1*. As you work through Book 2, you will find that your "keys" work better and better.

Unit *One*

FIVE STEPS FOR SOLVING PROBLEMS

Step One: Read the Problem

Aim: To read a word problem and reword the question

What You Need to Know

All word problems have two main parts. They contain **information** and a **question**. In the information part, you find the facts that you will use to answer the question. Before you begin to solve a word problem, you must make sure you *understand the question*.

So, Step 1 in solving any word problem is to—

- READ the problem. Get a general picture of what the problem is about.
- REREAD the problem more slowly. Focus on the details.
- REWORD the question. Put the question in your own words.

Think About It

Why do you think it helps to reword the question in a word problem?

_____

_____

Read and reread the following word problems. Then notice how the question is restated for each.

Example A The seventh- and eighth-grade students at Morris Junior High started a computer club. Altogether, 26 students attended the first meeting. Four more seventh-grade students attended the meeting than eighth-grade students. How many seventh-grade students attended the first meeting?

The Question: *How many seventh-grade students attended the first meeting?*

Example B The club voted to charge each member $5.75 to cover the cost of supplies. If 17 members pay the first week, how much money will be added to the club treasury?

The Question: *How much money will be collected?*

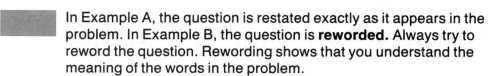

In Example A, the question is restated exactly as it appears in the problem. In Example B, the question is **reworded.** Always try to reword the question. Rewording shows that you understand the meaning of the words in the problem.

Practice

Read and reread each word problem. Then reword the question.

1. The club members voted to spend $30.00 to buy computer paper to print their programs. Each box of paper costs $13.88. How many boxes of paper will they be able to buy?

   The Question: _____

   _____

2. Laurie was 15 minutes early for the meeting. Ralph was 8 minutes late. How much later to the meeting was Ralph than Laurie?

   The Question: _____

   _____

3. The club members have set the following goal: Each member will write 3 new programs by the end of the first term. If all 26 club members meet the goal, how many new programs will be written by the end of the first term?

   The Question: _____

   _____

4. Mark spent $16\frac{1}{2}$ hours writing his first program. Carla spent $12\frac{3}{4}$ hours writing her first program. How many more hours did Mark spend than Carla?

   The Question: _____

   _____

5. Club members can use the school computers between 2:30 and 4:00 on Monday and Wednesday afternoons. They can use the computers between 1:15 and 3:00 Tuesday, Thursday, and Friday afternoons. What is the total number of hours the members can use the computers in 1 week?

   The Question: _____

   _____

Additional word problems for Lesson 1 skills practice are on page 83.

3

Lesson 2

Step Two: Find the Facts

Aim: To find the facts needed to solve a word problem

What You Need to Know

In Step 1, you read and reread the problem and then reword the question. In Step 2, you look at the other main part of the word problem. You look at the information part. You FIND THE FACTS needed to answer the question.

Often, a word problem will have extra information—facts you do not need. Keep the question in mind at all times. Decide which of the facts are important.

Many times, you can find all the needed facts "inside" the problem. Other times, you will have to look for facts "outside" the problem. You might find data in a diagram, a chart, a map, an appendix, or a dictionary. It doesn't matter where you find the facts as long as they help you to answer the question.

Think About It

Name three places "outside" a word problem where you may find needed facts.

_____

_____

Read each word problem below. Notice both the question and the facts needed to solve the problem. The question is underlined.

Example A The annual crafts street fair is open from 9 A.M. to 5 P.M. on Saturday and from 1 P.M. to 6 P.M. on Sunday. <u>How many hours is the fair open on Saturday?</u>

The Facts: *Time fair opens on Saturday: 9 A.M.*
Time fair closes on Saturday: 5 P.M.

Candy's Clay Creatures	
bugs	$1.25
dogs, cats	$3.95
horses	$4.95
dinosaurs	
large	$5.75
small	$3.45

Example B Candy made clay creatures to sell at the street fair. Marie bought 2 bugs and 3 small dinosaurs. <u>How much did Marie pay Candy?</u>

The Facts: *Number of bugs: 2*
Price of bugs: $1.25
Number of small dinosaurs: 3
Price of small dinosaurs: $3.45

4

In Example A, all the needed facts are "inside" the problem. In Example B, some of the needed facts are "outside" the problem, in a chart. Each problem contains extra information, facts that are *not* needed to solve the problem.

Practice

For each word problem, underline the question. Then write the facts you need to solve the problem. You may find the facts inside or outside the problem.

1. Molly made a hat for the street fair. To decorate the hat, she used 2.7 meters of pink ribbon, 1.5 meters of green ribbon, and 2.4 meters of white ribbon. How many meters of ribbon did she use in all?

   The Facts: _____

   _____

2. Frank drew a map to show Ben how to get to the fair. If Ben follows the map, how many blocks will he travel to the fair?

   The Facts: _____

   _____

3. Roberto made 6 plant hangers for the fair. He used $7\frac{1}{2}$ balls of blue cord and 72 beads. How many balls of cord did he use for each plant hanger?

   The Facts: _____

   _____

4. Rosa makes beaded necklaces. To make 1 of her best-selling necklaces, she needs 25 large black beads, 48 small black beads, and 24 silver beads. How many silver beads will Rosa need to make 8 of her best-selling necklaces?

   The Facts: _____

   _____

5. During the last hour of the fair, Candy sold 3 large dinosaurs to Ken for $4.50 each. How much did Ken save over the original price of the large dinosaurs? (Hint: Use the chart on page 4.)

   The Facts: _____

   _____

   _____

Ben's house

Maple St.

Elm Terrace

City Park

Oak St.

crafts
street fair

3

Step Three: Plan What to Do

Aim: To plan how to solve a word problem and, when possible, to estimate the answer

What You Need to Know

Once you know the question and find the needed facts, you can decide how to use the facts. In Step 3, you PLAN WHAT TO DO. Picture, or **visualize,** what is happening in the problem. This will help you to decide how to solve it.

For many problems, you will just need to compute. You will add, subtract, multiply, or divide. For other problems, you will use a different strategy. You may need to make a diagram, a table, or a graph. You may need to write an equation or use a formula. You may need some other strategy.

Once you have a plan, **estimate** the answer if you can. An estimate will help you to judge whether or not the final answer, when you get it, makes sense.

What will help you to choose a strategy for solving a problem?

Read the problems below. The question is underlined. There are circles around the needed facts. There is a label for the plan, such as "Add," followed by a description in parentheses.

At the library, 365 books were checked out on Monday. On Tuesday, 397 books were checked out. How many books were checked out on Monday and Tuesday?

The Plan: *Add (books checked out on Monday + books checked out on Tuesday = total books checked out on Monday and Tuesday)*

The Estimate: *350 + 400 = 750*

Rob volunteered to make a bulletin-board display for Book Week. The bulletin board is $12\frac{1}{2}$ feet wide and $6\frac{1}{2}$ feet long. How many square feet of space does Rob have for his display?

The Plan: *Use a formula: A = lw (area = length × width)*

The Estimate: *6 × 13 = 78*

In Example A, addition is used to solve the problem. In Example B, the formula for the area of a rectangle is needed *(A = lw)*. Formulas are included in the Appendix, on pages 120–122.

For each word problem, <u>underline</u> the question. (Circle) the needed facts. Then write a plan for solving the problem. Estimate the answer, if possible.

Suppose an average book in the library is 0.02 meter thick. How many meters of shelf space are needed for all 14,650 books?

The Plan: _____

_____

The Estimate: _____

The city is planning to repaint the baseboards along each wall in the main reading room of the library. The room is 27 feet wide and 52 feet long. How many feet of baseboard will be painted?

The Plan: _____

_____

The Estimate: _____

Ms. Garcia, the librarian, wants to buy a 15-volume set of science books and a 6-volume set of geography books. Each science book costs $24.95. Each geography book costs $32.75. How much will it cost to buy both complete sets of books? (Hint: Use two mathematical operations.)

The Plan: _____

_____

The Estimate: _____

The city is planning to carpet the reference area of the library. The carpet costs $10.95 per square yard. The reference area is 9 yards by 4 yards. How much will it cost to carpet the reference area? (Hint: Use two steps.)

The Plan: _____

_____

The Estimate: _____

Step Four: Carry Out the Plan

Aim: To carry out the plan for solving a word problem

What You Need to Know

In Step 3 of the problem solving process, you decide *how* to solve a word problem. In Step 4, you CARRY OUT THE PLAN.

Often, your plan, or **strategy,** for solving a problem will require computation. You can solve some problems mentally, in your head. For other problems, you will use paper and pencil or a calculator. Look at the numbers in each computation. Then decide which method will work best for you.

Think About It

Name three methods for computing a word problem.

_____

Read each word problem below. Notice how each step is completed. Step 1 is shown by underlining the question. Step 2 is shown by circling the needed facts. Step 3 is shown by labeling the plan and making an estimate. Step 4 is shown by carrying out, or executing, the plan.

Example A Rosa and Juan were hiking in Twin Lakes Park. They hiked for $3\frac{1}{4}$ hours. They stopped $1\frac{1}{4}$ hours for lunch. Then they continued hiking for $1\frac{2}{3}$ hours more. For how many hours did Rosa and Juan actually hike?

The Plan: *Add*		**The Estimate:** *3 + 2 = 5*

The Execution: $\quad 3\frac{1}{4} \qquad 3\frac{3}{12}$ **Answer:** $4\frac{11}{12}$ *hours*
(Use paper $\qquad \underline{+\ 1\frac{2}{3}} \quad \underline{+\ 1\frac{8}{12}}$
and pencil.) $\qquad\qquad\qquad\quad 4\frac{11}{12}$

Example B Altogether, 100 adults, 100 children between the ages of 6 and 18, and 53 children under 6 entered the park. How much money was collected?

The Plan: *Multiply and add*

The Estimate: *(100 × 2) + (100 × 1) = 300*

The Execution: *2.25*   *1.25*   *225*   **Answer:** *$350*
(Solve   *× 100*   *× 100*   *+ 125*
mentally.)   *225*   *125*   *350*

Twin Lakes Admission

Adults	$2.25
Children	
6–18 yrs	$1.25
under 6	free

In Example A, the problem can be solved using paper and pencil. In Example B, the problem can be solved mentally. In both problems, an estimated answer is found before computing.

Practice

For each problem, do each step as in the Examples. Show your computations in the space to the right of each item.

Hikers Snack Bar	
Hamburgers	$1.35
Peanuts	$0.45
Popcorn	$1.00
Fruit (apples, oranges, pears)	$0.75
Juice (orange, grapefruit, punch)	$0.85

1. Julie and Marge stopped for a snack as they entered the park. Julie got a hamburger and an orange juice. Marge got popcorn and an apple. What was the total bill?

   The Plan: _____

   The Estimate: _____   Answer: _____

   1. The Execution

2. The owners of the Hikers Snack Bar are hoping to sell 100 hamburgers today. If they reach their goal, how much money will they take in on the sale of hamburgers?

   The Plan: _____

   The Estimate: _____   Answer: _____

   2. The Execution

3. There are $44\frac{3}{4}$ km of hiking trails in Twin Lakes Park. Cody hiked $10\frac{1}{4}$ km on Monday. He hiked $11\frac{3}{4}$ km on Tuesday and $14\frac{3}{4}$ km on Wednesday. How much farther did he hike on Wednesday than on Monday?

   The Plan: _____

   The Estimate: _____   Answer: _____

   3. The Execution

4. Abe, Rosita, Carrie, Dave, and Eric bought 12.5 kg of food to take on their hiking trip. Each person carried the same amount of food. How much weight in food did each person carry?

   The Plan: _____

   The Estimate: _____   Answer: _____

   4. The Execution

Additional word problems for Lesson 4 skills practice are on page 86.

9

Step Five: Check the Answer

Aim: To check the answer to a word problem

What You Need to Know

It may be tempting to go through the first four steps, get an answer, and stop there. Don't give in to the temptation! Step 5 is a very important step. You need to CHECK THE ANSWER.

Checking the answer means two things. First, check that the answer is **reasonable.** (Does it make sense? Does it answer the question? Is it close to the estimate you made in Step 3?) Second, check for **computation accuracy.**

Think About It

Why, do you think, is Step 5 one of the most important steps?

_____

_____

Read each problem below. Notice the check that is used to decide if the answer is correct.

Example A During a track meet, David ran the 100-yard dash in 10.6 seconds. Joshua ran the same distance in 9.8 seconds. How much faster was Joshua's time than David's time?

The Plan: *Subtract*   **The Estimate:** *11 − 10 = 1*

The Execution: *10.6*   **Answer:** *0.9 second*
     − 9.8
     0.9

The Check: *Is answer reasonable? Yes.*
     Does computation check? No. (Computing "backward" shows 9.8 + 0.9 = 10.7, not 10.6.)

Example B During practice, Joyce ran the 100-yard dash twice. She ran it in 11.3 seconds and in 10.2 seconds. What was Joyce's average time during practice?

The Plan: *Add*   **The Estimate:** *11 + 10 = 21*

The Execution: *11.3*   **Answer:** *21.5 seconds*
     + 10.2
     21.5

The Check: *Is answer reasonable? No. (How can an average time be longer than any single time?)*

In Example A, the answer is reasonable. It makes sense; it answers the question; it is close to the estimate. However, the computation does not check. The correct answer is 0.8 second.

In Example B, the answer is not reasonable. Whether or not the computation checks, you need to reread the problem. You may need to choose a different plan. In Example B, the plan needs to be "Add and divide." The correct answer is 10.75 seconds.

Practice

For each problem, study how Steps 3 and 4 were done. Then show the two-part check to decide if the answer is correct. If it is not, correct it.

1. During a 1-mile relay race, Pete ran the first lap in 84.6 seconds. Rosa ran the second lap in 93.4 seconds. Tom ran the third lap in 87.8 seconds. How long did it take them to run the mile?

   The Plan: Add   The Estimate: 85 + 90 + 90 = 265
   The Execution: 84.6   Answer: 268.8 seconds, or
                      93.4   4 min. 48 sec.
                    + 87.8
                      268.8

   The Check: _____

   _____

2. In two practices, Lynn pole-vaulted 9.6 feet and 10.7 feet. By how many feet did she better the height from the first to the second vault?

   The Plan: Subtract   The Estimate: 11 − 10 = 1
   The Execution: 10.7   Answer: 20.3 feet
                   − 9.6
                    20.3

   The Check: _____

   _____

3. Maria practiced for the track meet for $1\frac{1}{2}$ hours each on Monday, Wednesday, and Friday. She practiced for $2\frac{1}{4}$ hours each on Tuesday and Thursday. For how many hours did Maria practice in all?

   The Plan: Multiply and add   The Estimate: 5 × 2 = 10
   The Execution: $1\frac{1}{2}$ $2\frac{1}{4}$ $4\frac{1}{2}$ Answer: 9 hours
                    × 3   × 2   + $4\frac{1}{2}$
                    $4\frac{1}{2}$ $4\frac{1}{2}$ 9

   The Check: _____

   _____

Additional word problems for Lesson 5 skills practice are on page 87.

Lesson 6

Cumulative Practice: Steps 1, 2, 3, 4, and 5

Aim: To practice with Steps 1, 2, 3, 4, and 5 in combination

What You Need to Know

To review the five steps for solving any word problem, look at the top of the next page. Like the best teacher you ever had, these steps will never steer you wrong. They are a guide to success.

You may find that you can already do some of the steps mentally, in your head. There's nothing wrong with that! Just be sure *never to skip a step.* Each one is important to getting the right answer.

Think About It

Think about your own work with word problems in this unit. Where have you been most likely to make a mistake? Which step helps you to stay on the right track?

_____

_____

Read the Example. Notice how all five steps are followed.

Example For a woodworking project, Janice cut two pieces from a board. She cut off a ⟨22⅜-inch⟩ piece and a ⟨10⅝-inch⟩ piece. A ⟨38-inch⟩ piece of board was left. How long was the board originally?

The Question Reworded: *How long was the board before she cut the pieces?* (Question is underlined.)

The Facts: *Board lengths: 22⅜ inches, 10⅝ inches, 38 inches* (Needed facts are circled.)

The Plan: *Add*   **The Estimate:** *20 + 10 + 40 = 70*

The Execution: $22\frac{3}{8}$ **Answer:** *71 inches*
$$10\frac{5}{8}$$
$$\underline{+\ 38}$$
$$71$$

The Check: *Answer is reasonable.* (It answers the question, makes sense, and is close to the estimate.)
   Computation is correct. (Adding the numbers in a different order gives the same answer.)

The Example serves as a review of the five-step process for solving word problems. Be sure you have thought through the Example carefully before doing the Practice items below.

Practice

For each problem below, <u>underline</u> the question and (circle) the needed facts. Then write the plan and estimate the answer. Finally, carry out the plan and check the answer.

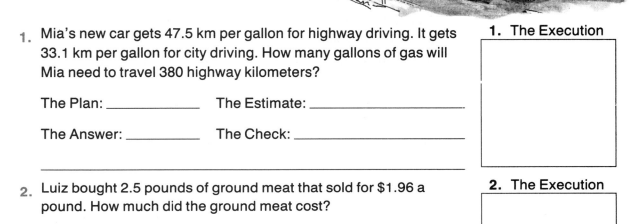

1. Mia's new car gets 47.5 km per gallon for highway driving. It gets 33.1 km per gallon for city driving. How many gallons of gas will Mia need to travel 380 highway kilometers?

    The Plan: _____ The Estimate: _____

    The Answer: _____ The Check: _____

    _____

    1. The Execution

2. Luiz bought 2.5 pounds of ground meat that sold for $1.96 a pound. How much did the ground meat cost?

    The Plan: _____ The Estimate: _____

    The Answer: _____ The Check: _____

    _____

    2. The Execution

3. Beth bought a camera for $57.95. She bought 2 rolls of film for $3.89 each. What was her total bill?

    The Plan: _____ The Estimate: _____

    The Answer: _____ The Check: _____

    _____

    3. The Execution

4. A local TV station begins the day with a 45-minute program of news and health tips. The news takes $11\frac{1}{2}$ minutes. How much time is left for health tips?

    The Plan: _____ The Estimate: _____

    The Answer: _____ The Check: _____

    _____

    4. The Execution

Unit 1 Review

On each line, write **T** or **F** to tell whether the statement is true or false.

_____ 1. Before you begin to solve a word problem, you must make sure you understand the question.

_____ 2. If you can reword the question in a word problem, it means you have solved the problem.

_____ 3. The facts needed to solve a word problem are always found "inside" the words of the problem.

_____ 4. Sometimes a word problem has extra information—facts that are not needed to solve the problem.

_____ 5. Visualizing what is happening in a problem may help you to decide how to solve the problem.

_____ 6. All you need to know to solve any word problem is how to add, subtract, multiply, or divide.

_____ 7. The plan for solving a word problem is called a _strategy._

_____ 8. Using a calculator is the best method for solving all word problems.

_____ 9. When checking an answer, you should first check that the answer is reasonable and then check that the computation is accurate.

_____ 10. As a general rule, it is okay to skip a problem solving step to save time.

On each line, write the word that best completes the sentence.

_____ 11. The two main parts of any word problem are information and a _____.

_____ 12. In Step 2 of the problem solving process, you find the _____ you need to answer the question.

_____ 13. Once you have a plan for solving a problem, it is a good idea to _____ the answer; this will help you judge whether the final answer, when you get it, makes sense.

_____ 14. After you decide how to solve a word problem, you are ready to _____ the plan.

_____ 15. The last step in solving any word problem is to _____ the answer.

Circle the letter of the correct answer.

Kevin is learning to play the guitar. His brother plays the piano. A guitar lesson is $\frac{1}{2}$ hour long and costs $7.25. A book of music costs $3.95. How much does Kevin pay for 5 guitar lessons?

Which of these is a rewording of the question in the problem above?
a. How much do 5 books of music cost?
b. How much more does a guitar lesson cost than a book of music?
c. How much does it cost Kevin for 5 guitar lessons?
d. How much do a guitar lesson and a book of music cost?

Which of these is a needed fact for solving the problem above?
a. A book of music costs $3.95.
b. Guitar lessons cost $7.25 each.
c. A guitar lesson lasts $\frac{1}{2}$ hour.
d. Kevin's brother takes piano lessons.

Which of these is a plan for solving the word problem above?
a. Add (price of guitar lesson + price of book)
b. Multiply (5 × price of books)
c. Subtract (price of guitar lessons − price of book)
d. Multiply (5 × price of guitar lesson)

Which of these shows a way to estimate the answer to the problem above?
a. 5 × 7 = 35   b. 5 × 4 = 20   c. 7 − 4 = 3   d. 7 + 4 = 11

To decorate a costume, Amy used $3\frac{3}{4}$ yards of blue ribbon and $2\frac{1}{2}$ yards of yellow ribbon. How much ribbon did she use in all?
a. $6\frac{1}{4}$ yards   b. $5\frac{1}{4}$ yards   c. $5\frac{4}{6}$ yards   d. $6\frac{1}{2}$ yards

Wendy drove 418 miles on Monday and 279 miles on Tuesday. How much farther did she drive on Monday than on Tuesday?
a. 697 miles   b. 261 miles   c. 139 miles   d. 249 miles

Todd bought 3 cans of tennis balls. The total bill was $8.37. How much did he pay for each can of tennis balls?
a. $0.28   b. $25.11   c. $27.90   d. $2.79

There are 28 students in Ms. Went's class. Each student is writing a 9-page science report. How many pages will Ms. Went have to read?

Which of these is NOT a reasonable answer to the problem above?
a. 262 pages   b. 625 pages   c. 252 pages   d. 272 pages

Which of these is the correct answer to the problem above?
a. 262 pages   b. 625 pages   c. 252 pages   d. 272 pages

Which of these shows a way to check the computation for the problem above?
a.   252   b.   28   c.   28   d. 9)252
   − 28   + 9   − 9

D. Read and reread each word problem. Then follow the directions to show your solution to the problem.

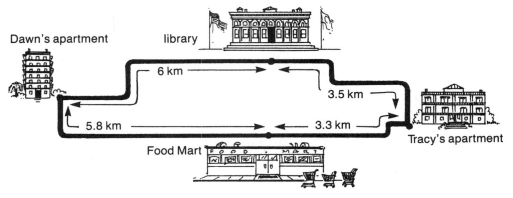

26. From her apartment, Dawn roller-skated past the Food Mart to Tracy's apartment. How many kilometers did she skate in all?
    a. Underline the question.
    b. Circle the needed facts in the problem.

    c. Describe your plan: _____

    _____

    d. If an estimate can be made, show it here: _____

    e. Carry out your plan. Answer: _____

    f. Check your answer. If you got an incorrect answer, tell how you know it is wrong. Then write the correct answer.

    _____

    _____

27. The school football team is buying 12 new helmets and 8 new footballs. Helmets cost $89 each, and footballs cost $35 each. How much will the team spend on new helmets?
    a. Underline the question.
    b. Circle the needed facts in the problem.

    c. Describe your plan: _____

    _____

    d. If an estimate can be made, show it here: _____

    e. Carry out your plan. Answer: _____

    f. Check your answer. If you got an incorrect answer, tell how you know it is wrong. Then write the correct answer.

    _____

    _____

Unit *Two*

DEVELOPING YOUR PROBLEM SOLVING SKILLS

Too Much or Too Little Information

Aim: To recognize when a problem contains unneeded facts or not enough facts

What You Need to Know

Problems in your daily life will rarely come with just the right amount of information. Often, there are extra, unimportant facts that you do not need to solve the problem. Other times, there may be too few facts to solve the problem.

Remember, your first task when solving any word problem is to be sure you *understand the question.* Then decide what facts you need to solve the problem. You may need to look both "inside" and "outside" the problem for the facts. Ask yourself, "Which of the given facts are needed to solve the problem? Are any important facts missing?" To solve the problem, you must have all the needed facts.

Think About It

When solving any word problem, what must you do before you can decide what facts you need?

Read the word problems below. Notice the needed data. In each problem, there are circles around the important facts. The unnecessary facts are crossed out. If there is a missing fact, it is described.

Example A   A tray holds (60 cookies) and a plate holds ~~24 cookies~~. If there are (5 trays) of cookies, how many cookies are on trays?
Missing Fact: *None*
The Execution: 60   **Answer:** *300 cookies*
$$\begin{array}{r} 60 \\ \times\ 5 \\ \hline 300 \end{array}$$

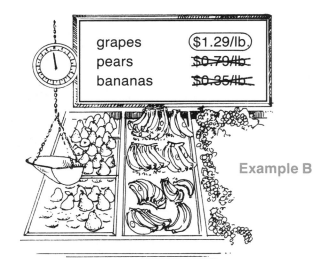

grapes	($1.29/lb.)
pears	~~$0.79/lb.~~
bananas	~~$0.35/lb.~~

Example B   Grapes, pears, and bananas are sold by the pound at Ace's Supermarket. Betty bought a bag of grapes. How much did she pay for the bag of grapes?
Missing Fact: *Number of pounds of grapes in the bag*
The Execution: *The problem cannot be solved.*

In Example A, there is one unneeded fact. You don't need to know how many cookies a plate will hold. That unnecessary fact is crossed out. There are no missing facts in the problem, so the problem can be solved.

In Example B, there is both unneeded information (the price per pound for pears and bananas) and missing information. To solve the problem, you would need to know how many pounds of grapes were in the bag. This problem cannot be solved with the facts given.

Practice

For each problem, underline the question and reword it to yourself. Circle the needed data. Cross out the unnecessary data. If all the needed facts are given, solve the problem. If there is a missing fact, describe it as was done in Example B.

1. Lori is practicing for the track team. Each Tuesday, Thursday, and Saturday, she jogs $1\frac{1}{2}$ miles and does 25 leg lifts. On Monday, Wednesday, and Friday, she jogs $2\frac{1}{2}$ miles. How many leg lifts does Lori do in a week?

_____

2. Sailing classes are held Monday and Thursday afternoon. If both classes are full, how many people are taking sailing lessons?

_____

3. In the local library, $\frac{2}{5}$ of the books are nonfiction and $\frac{3}{5}$ of the books are fiction. How many fiction books are in the library?

_____

4. Luiz and Franco went fishing for 4 hours. They caught 5 bass and 6 catfish. Each catfish weighed 3 pounds. How many pounds of catfish did they catch?

_____

5. In a swimming relay, Karla swam her lap in 45.4 seconds. Joe swam his lap in 42.6 seconds. Kim swam her lap in 39.7 seconds. How much faster did Kim swim than Karla?

_____

Lesson 8

Reading a Map

Aim: To locate needed facts on a map

What You Need to Know

Sometimes the facts you need to solve a problem are found in a map. When you need to find data on a map, first study the *whole* map. Get an overall idea of what is included. Read the title of the map. Notice the kinds of places marked on the map. Find out how distances are shown on the map.

When you are solving a problem with a map, do the following:

- First, read the problem and understand the question.
- Second, study the map.
- Third, reread the problem while you locate the needed facts on the map.

Think About It

Why should you study the whole map before trying to find the needed facts?

Read the word problems below. Notice where the facts needed to solve the problem are located.

Driving Distances between California Cities
(All distances are in miles.)

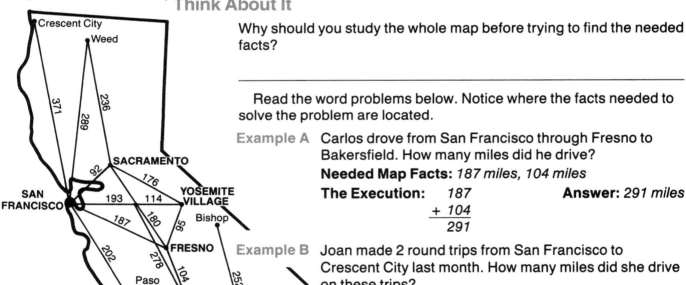

Example A   Carlos drove from San Francisco through Fresno to Bakersfield. How many miles did he drive?
Needed Map Facts: *187 miles, 104 miles*

The Execution:	187	**Answer:** *291 miles*
	+ 104	
	291	

Example B   Joan made 2 round trips from San Francisco to Crescent City last month. How many miles did she drive on these trips?
Needed Map Facts: *371 miles*

The Execution:	371	**Answer:** *1,484 miles*
	× 4	
	1,484	

In both Examples A and B, the data needed to solve the problems are on the map. In Example B, there is also a piece of data "inside" the word problem. It tells you that Joan made "2 round trips." Each round trip would include a 371-mile trip from San Francisco to Crescent City *and* a 371-mile return trip from Crescent City back to San Francisco. Therefore, Joan would make four 371-mile trips in all.

Practice

For each problem, write the facts you will use from the map. Write the plan and the answer. (Remember to follow all five steps!) Use the map on page 20 for items 1 and 2.

1. How much farther is it from Los Angeles to San Diego than it is from Los Angeles to Santa Barbara? Use the shortest distances possible.

   Needed Map Facts: _____

   The Plan: _____   Answer: _____

2. It took Juan 4 hours to drive from San Francisco to Paso Robles. He drove the same number of miles each hour. How many miles did Juan drive each hour?

   Needed Map Facts: _____

   The Plan: _____   Answer: _____

**Driving Distances
between Tennessee and
North Carolina Cities**
(All distances are in miles.)

NASHVILLE 177 KNOXVILLE   TENN. GREENSBORO Durham 27 51 154 Nags Head
132   133   118   175   54   Raleigh   Rocky Mount   N.C.
87 Jackson   111   Asheville 113   94   CHARLOTTE   131
MEMPHIS 320 CHATTANOOGA   TENN. N.C.   124 Lumberton   211
73 Wilmington

3. Billy drove from his home in Asheville through Charlotte to Greensboro. How many miles did he drive in all?

   Needed Map Facts: _____

   The Plan: _____   Answer: _____

4. Julie drove from Memphis through Nashville to Chattanooga. Debbie drove the shortest route from Memphis to Chattanooga. How many more miles did Julie drive than Debbie?

   Needed Map Facts: _____

   The Plan: _____   Answer: _____

Additional word problems for Lesson 8 skills practice are on page 90.

21

9

Reading a Table

Aim: To locate needed facts in a table or chart

What You Need to Know

A table organizes all the numbers you see on bus, train, and airline **schedules.** With a table, you can find pieces of information quickly. The first thing to do is read the title and any headings. These will give you an overall understanding. Then look for the facts you need.

Read the title and heading in the table below. Where does the 6:10 A.M. train from Cedarton stop before reaching Oaksbury?

Read the Examples. Notice where the needed facts are found.

Commuter Train Schedule							
Cedarton to Oaksbury				Oaksbury to Cedarton			
Departs			**Arrives**	**Departs**		**Arrives**	
Cedarton	Appleville	Wilson	Oaksbury	Oaksbury	Wilson	Appleville	Cedarton
6:10 A.M.	6:15 A.M.	6.25 A.M.	6.57 A.M.	9:30 A.M.	10:03 A.M.	10.13 A.M.	10:18 A.M.
7:10 A.M.	—	7:22 A.M.	7:54 A.M.	11:45 A.M.	—	12:25 P. M.	12:30 P. M.
8:30 A.M.	8:35 A.M.	8:45 P. M.	9:17 A.M.	3:20 P. M.	3:53 P. M.	4:03 P. M.	4:08 P. M.
11:20 A.M.	11:25 A.M.	—	12:04 P. M.	5:10 P. M.	5:43 P. M.	5:53 P. M.	5:58 P. M.
3.15 P. M.	3:20 P. M.	3:40 P. M.	4:12 P. M.	6:20 P. M.	6:53 P. M.	7:03 P. M.	7:08 P. M.
6:30 P. M.	6:35 P. M.	6:45 P. M.	7:17 P. M.	6:45 P. M.	7:18 P. M.	—	7:30 P. M.
8:45 P. M.	8:50 P. M.	9:00 P. M.	9:32 P. M.	8:10 P. M.	8:43 P. M.	8:53 P. M.	8:58 P. M.

Amy commutes to work by train from Cedarton to Oaksbury every day. If she rides the 7:10 A.M. train, how long does it take her to get to Oaksbury?

Needed Table Facts: *7:10 A.M.; 7:54 A.M.*

The Execution: *7 hr. 54 min.*   **Answer:** *44 minutes*
                       − 7 hr. 10 min.
                       44 min.

Amy takes the 6:20 P.M. train home from Oaksbury to Cedarton. After leaving the train, she still has a 12-minute walk. What time does she get home?

Needed Table Facts: *7:08 P.M.*

The Execution: *7 hr.   8 min.*   **Answer:** *7:20 P.M.*
                   + 12 min.
                   7 hr. 20 min.

For Example A, look for the train that leaves Cedarton at 7:10 A.M.
For Example B, look for the train leaving Oaksbury at 6:20 P.M.

Write the facts you will use from the table. Then write the plan and the answer. Use the schedule on page 22 for items 1, 2, and 3.

Blanca took the 5:10 P.M. train from Oaksbury to Appleville. How long was her train ride?

Needed Table Facts: _____

The Plan: _____   Answer: _____

One morning, the 7:10 A.M. train from Cedarton was 15 minutes late arriving at Oaksbury. What time did it get there?

Needed Table Facts: _____

The Plan: _____   Answer: _____

Dave rides to work on the 6:25 A.M. train from Wilson to Oaksbury 5 days a week. How much time does he spend commuting to work on the train in 1 week?

Needed Table Facts: _____

The Plan: _____   Answer: _____

North-Bound Bus Schedule							
Leave							**Arrive**
North Port	Englewood	So. County Courthouse Annex	Venice Hospital	Venice	Nokomis	Osprey	Sarasota Sq. Mall
7:15 A.M.	7:35 A.M.	7:50 A.M.	8:00 A.M.	8:05 A.M.	8:10 A.M.	8:15 A.M.	8:25 A.M.
9:45 A.M.	10:05 A.M.	10:20 A.M.	10:30 A.M.	10:35 A.M.	10:40 A.M.	10:45 A.M.	10:55 A.M.
12:45 P.M.	1:05 P.M.	1:20 P.M.	1:30 P.M.	1:35 P.M.	1:40 P.M.	1:45 P.M.	1:55 P.M.
3:15 P.M.	3:35 P.M.	3:50 P.M.	4:00 P.M.	4:05 P.M.	4:10 P.M.	4:15 P.M.	4:25 P.M.
5:45 P.M.	6:05 P.M.	6:20 P.M.	6:30 P.M.	6:35 P.M.	6:40 P.M.	6:50 P.M.	6:55 P.M.
—	—	—	—	7:20 P.M.	7:25 P.M.	7:30 P.M.	7:35 P.M.

Nathan caught the 10:30 A.M. bus at Venice Hospital and rode to Sarasota Square Mall. How long was his bus ride?

Needed Table Facts: _____

The Plan: _____   Answer: _____

The bus that leaves North Port at 5:45 P.M. was 23 minutes late arriving at Osprey. What time did the bus arrive at Osprey?

Needed Table Facts: _____

The Plan: _____   Answer: _____

Reading a Graph

Aim: To locate needed facts in a line graph

What You Need to Know

 Sometimes you will find needed facts in a graph. A **line graph** can show change over time. If there is a *trend* (a steady increase, decrease, or period of no change), this can be seen easily. The steeper the line, the sharper the increase or decrease.

Read the title and all labels on a graph before you begin to look for specific data. Be sure you understand the *intervals,* or units, that are used along both scales of the graph.

Think About It

Read the labels on the graph on this page. What do the numbers

along the left side of the graph represent? _____

What is shown along the bottom of the graph? _____

Read the Example below. Notice where the facts are found.

Example

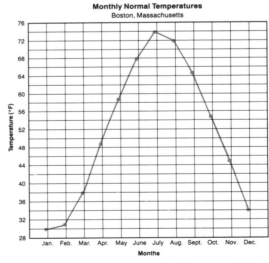

How many degrees warmer is the monthly normal temperature in Boston in July than in January?

Needed Graph Facts: *74 degrees; 30 degrees*

The Execution: 74
                    − 30
                    ‾‾‾‾
                      44

Answer: *44 degrees*

In the Example, the needed facts are found in the line graph. Notice that the line from January to February goes almost straight across. This shows that the normal temperature is about the same (30–31°F) for these two months. The line goes up steeply from February to July. This shows a sharp *increase* in the normal temperature. The line goes down from July to December. This shows a *decrease* in the normal temperature.

Practice

For each problem, write the facts you will use from the graph. Then write the plan and the answer. (Follow all five problem solving steps.) Use the graph on page 24 for items 1 and 2.

1. In Boston, how many degrees colder is the normal temperature in March than in April?

   Needed Graph Facts: _____

   The Plan: _____   Answer: _____

2. One day in August, the temperature went 13 degrees above normal for August. How high did the temperature go on that day?

   Needed Graph Facts: _____

   The Plan: _____   Answer: _____

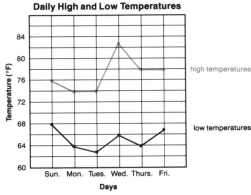

3. How many degrees warmer was the high temperature on Wednesday than the high temperature on Monday?

   Needed Graph Facts: _____

   The Plan: _____   Answer: _____

4. Forecasters are predicting that the high temperature on Saturday will be 6 degrees higher than the high temperature on Friday. What is the high temperature on Saturday predicted to be?

   Needed Graph Facts: _____

   The Plan: _____   Answer: _____

Using the Appendix

Aim: To locate needed facts in an appendix

What You Need to Know

Sometimes, needed facts are not only "outside" the problem—they're not even on the problem page! When this happens, ask yourself, "Where can I find that fact?" Remember, it doesn't matter *where* you find it, as long as you find it.

The fact you need may be on a calendar, in an almanac, in a dictionary, or on another page in your math book. To solve the problems in this lesson, you will find needed data in the Appendix, on pages 120–122.

Think About It

Name the types of facts that are found in this book's Appendix.

_____

_____

Read the problems below. Check the Appendix for each problem to see where the data are found.

Example A A nail weighs about 2 grams. About how many nails are in a bag that weighs 1 kilogram?

Needed Appendix Facts: *1 kg = 1,000 g*

The Execution: $\frac{500}{2\overline{)1,000}}$ **Answer:** *about 500 nails*

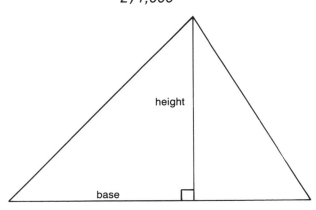

height

base

Example B Find the area of a triangle with a base of 8 cm and a height of 5 cm.

Needed Appendix Facts: $A = \frac{1}{2}bh$

The Execution: $\frac{1}{2} \times 8 \times 5 = 20$ **Answer:** *20 cm²*

The facts needed to solve both Examples A and B can be found in the Appendix. In Example A, you need to convert kilograms to grams. In Example B, you need to find the formula for the area of a triangle.

Practice

For each problem, write the facts you will use from the Appendix. Then write the plan and the answer. Use 3.14 for π. Remember to follow all five problem solving steps, including the check on your answer.

1. The diameter of a bicycle wheel is 52 centimeters. What is the circumference of this bicycle wheel?

   Needed Appendix Facts: _____

   Answer: _____

2. A developer owns $2\frac{1}{2}$ square miles of land. How many acres does she own?

   Needed Appendix Facts: _____

   Answer: _____

3. Ralph is carpeting his living room and dining room. He needs 182 square feet of carpet for the living room. He needs 106 square feet of carpet for the dining room. How many square yards of carpet does he need in all?

   Needed Appendix Facts: _____

   Answer: _____

4. This aquarium is a rectangular prism. Find its volume.

   Needed Appendix Facts: _____

   Answer: _____

5. A truck carrying 6 metric tons of freight made deliveries to 4 warehouses. Each warehouse received the same amount of freight. How many kilograms of freight did each warehouse receive?

   Needed Appendix Facts: _____

   Answer: _____

Additional word problems for Lesson 11 skills practice are on page 93.

27

Lesson 12

Choosing the Operation

Aim: To understand when to add, subtract, multiply, or divide to solve a word problem

What You Need to Know

Many word problems are *routine.* You simply add, subtract, multiply, or divide to solve them. To choose the operation, *visualize* the action. Study the chart below.

Once you know the operation, then choose the best way to compute. The best way may be mentally, with paper and pencil, or with a calculator. Remember to estimate your answer first.

Choose the Operation

Action	Operation
Joining different-sized groups (a different number in each group) to find a total	Addition
Separating Objects to find a group that is left or **Comparing two groups** to find the difference	Subtraction
Joining equal groups to find a total	Multiplication
Sharing equally to find the size of each group or **Making groups of a given size** to find the number of groups	Division

Think About It

Why is it a good idea to estimate an answer before computing it?

Read each problem below. Visualize the action.

Example A There are 231 students going by bus to the Natural History Museum. Each bus holds 66 people. How many buses are needed?

The Action: *Making groups of a given size*

The Execution:
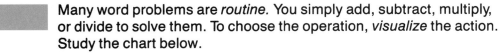
$$66)\overline{231} \quad 3\tfrac{1}{2}$$

Answer: *4 buses*

Example B At the museum gift shop, Marie bought a book for $2.95 and a pin for $1.79. How much did she spend in all?

The Action: *Joining different-sized groups*

The Execution:
$$\begin{array}{r} 2.95 \\ + 1.79 \\ \hline 4.74 \end{array}$$

Answer: *$4.74*

After "The Action" heading in each Example, a short version of the whole section from the chart is listed. Notice that the answer in Example A is $3\frac{1}{2}$. It is not possible to hire half a bus. The quotient must be rounded up, to 4.

Remember, when you have a **remainder** in the quotient, you need to decide how to "show" it in your answer. Read the problem again. Decide how to **interpret** the remainder. Show the computed mixed-number answer. Or, show the quotient rounded up or down to the next whole number. Or, show the remainder by itself.

Practice

For each problem, visualize the action. Then write the action, the operation, and the answer. (Be sure to check your answers. Do they agree with your estimates? Do they make sense?)

1. Going to the museum, the bus driver followed a route that was 17.5 km and took 25 minutes. On the way back, the driver took a route that was 15.9 km and took 20 minutes. How much farther was the trip to the museum than from the museum?

    The Action: _____

    The Operation: _____   Answer: _____

2. The museum takes $7\frac{1}{2}$ hours to show a movie 6 times with no time between showings. How long is the movie?

    The Action: _____

    The Operation: _____   Answer: _____

3. There were 211 students and 20 adults on the trip. What was the total cost of admission for the students?

    The Action: _____

    The Operation: _____   Answer: _____

4. Posters at the museum cost $2.10 each. Paulo has $7.35. How many posters can he buy?

    The Action: _____

    The Operation: _____   Answer: _____

5. The museum has a special exhibit on the Ice Age. On Saturday, 937 people saw the exhibit. On Sunday, 895 people saw it. How many people saw the exhibit during the weekend?

    The Action: _____

    The Operation: _____   Answer: _____

Museum Admission	
Adults	$7.50
Students	$4.25
Children under 6	free

Additional word problems for Lesson 12 skills practice are on page 94.

Two-Operation Problems

Aim: To solve problems that involve two operations

What You Need to Know

Often, you will need to use two operations to solve a problem. Such a problem has a main question and a "hidden" question. Follow the same five problem solving steps, this time twice.

Step 1: As always, read the problem and reword the main question. Decide what the hidden question is.

Now follow Steps 2–5 to answer the hidden question.

Step 2: Find the needed facts. **Step 4:** Carry out the plan.
Step 3: Plan what to do. **Step 5:** Check the answer.

Once you answer the hidden question, repeat Steps 2–5 to answer the main question. Your answer to the hidden question is part of the data you need in Step 2.

Think About It

In a two-operation problem, why must you do all the steps twice?

Calorie Chart	
Food	**Calories**
Apple, raw	117
Banana, fresh	119
Bread (1 slice)	
White	60
Whole Wheat	55
Butter (1 pat)	50
Cantaloupe (whole)	74
Cheese (1 slice)	
American	115
Swiss	105
Cheese (1 cup)	
Cottage	216
Chicken, roasted	
(1 slice)	79
Egg, boiled	77
Flounder (4 oz.)	78
Grapefruit	208
Milk (1 cup)	
Skim	87
Whole	165
Muffin, blueberry	125
Orange	106
Peach	35
Potato, baked	97
Strawberries, fresh	
(1 cup)	54
Turkey, roasted	
(1 slice)	100
Yogurt (1 cup)	
Skim milk	120

Read each Example. The first operation is used for the hidden question. The second operation is used for the main question.

Example A Beth used 2 slices of whole wheat bread and 1 slice of roast chicken. How many calories are in the sandwich?

Hidden Question: *How many calories are in 2 slices of whole wheat bread?*

First Operation:	Second Operation:	Answer
Multiplication	*Addition*	**to Main**
55	110	**Question:**
× 2	+ 79	*189 calories*
110	189	

Example B Brian sliced 7 peaches to make dessert for 5 people. About how many calories were in each serving?

Hidden Question: *How many calories are in 7 peaches?*

First Operation:	Second Operation:	Answer
Multiplication	*Division*	**to Main**
35	49	**Question:**
× 7	5)245	*about 49*
245		*calories*

In Example A, you *multiply* to find the answer to the hidden question. Then you *add* that answer to the number of calories in 1 slice of chicken. This gives you the answer to the main question. In Example B, you *multiply* to find the answer to the hidden question. Then you *divide* that answer to find the answer to the main question.

Practice

For each problem, write the names of the two operations you will use. Then solve the problem. Be sure to follow the five steps to answer both the hidden and the main questions.

1. Susan usually drinks 5 cups of whole milk each day. How many fewer calories would she consume if she drank 5 cups of skim milk?

   First Operation: _____   Answer:

   Second Operation: _____   _____

2. Ricky used 3 cups of strawberries, 4 oranges, and 5 apples to make a fruit salad. How many calories are in the fruit salad?

   First Operation: _____   Answer:

   Second Operation: _____   _____

3. Joanne ate a 455-calorie breakfast, a 379-calorie lunch, and a 726-calorie dinner. What was the *average* number of calories she consumed at each meal?

   First Operation: _____   Answer:

   Second Operation: _____   _____

4. Jeff used $\frac{1}{3}$ cup cottage cheese and $\frac{1}{2}$ cantaloupe to make an after-school snack. How many calories were in his snack?

   First Operation: _____   Answer:

   Second Operation: _____   _____

5. Lewis usually eats a banana and an apple with his lunch. Today he ate a peach and a grapefruit instead. How many more calories did he consume in today's fruit?

   First Operation: _____   Answer:

   Second Operation: _____   _____

Lesson 14

Multiple-Step Problems

Aim: To solve problems that have more than one "hidden" question

What You Need to Know

Now you will solve problems with more than one "hidden" question. Thus, you will follow the five steps *more* than two times. These are **multiple-step problems.** You need to answer two or three hidden questions before you can answer the main question.

Think About It

In which step do you find the hidden questions? _____

Read each problem below. Notice the order in which the operations are used.

Example A   Mandy is painting the 4 walls in her hobby shop. Each wall is 8.5 m long and 3.2 m high. A can of paint covers about 40 m². How many cans of paint does Mandy need to buy to give each wall one coat of paint?

Hidden Questions in Example A:
1. *What is the area of one wall?*
2. *What is the total area of four walls?*

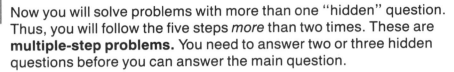

First Operation: *Multiplication*
(Hidden Question 1)

$$\begin{array}{r} 3.2 \\ \times\ 8.5 \\ \hline 27.2 \end{array}$$

Second Operation: *Multiplication*
(Hidden Question 2)

$$\begin{array}{r} 27.2 \\ \times\ 4 \\ \hline 108.8 \end{array}$$

Answer to Main Question:
3 cans of paint

Third Operation: *Division*
(Main Question)

$$40)\overline{108.8} \quad 2.72$$

Example B   Mandy bought a computer for 15% off the list price. The list price was $695. Mandy made a $200 down payment. She agreed to pay the rest in 5 equal monthly payments. What were her monthly payments?

Hidden Questions in Example B:
1. *How much did she save off the list price?*
2. *How much did she pay for the computer?*
3. *How much did she pay altogether in monthly payments?*

First Operation: *Multiplication*
(Hidden Question 1)

$$\begin{array}{r} 695 \\ \times\ .15 \\ \hline 104.25 \end{array}$$

Second Operation: *Subtraction*
(Hidden Question 2)

$$\begin{array}{r} 695.00 \\ -\ 104.25 \\ \hline 590.75 \end{array}$$

Third Operation: *Subtraction*
(Hidden Question 3)

$$\begin{array}{r} 590.75 \\ -\ 200.00 \\ \hline 390.75 \end{array}$$

Answer to Main Question:
$78.15

Fourth Operation: *Division*
(Main Question)

$$5)\overline{390.75} \quad 78.15$$

In Example A, there are two hidden questions and three operations. The first operation answers the first hidden question. The second operation answers the second one. The third operation answers the main question. In Example B, there are three hidden questions and four operations.

In Example A, Mandy cannot buy part of a can of paint. Interpret the remainder by rounding up to the next whole number.

Practice

For each problem, write the order of operations you will use. Then solve the problem. Be sure to check *all* your answers.

1. Gary bought 3 model airplanes and 2 tubes of glue at the hobby shop. Each tube of glue cost $2.59. The total bill was $21.95. What was the average price Gary paid for the models?

   First: _____   Second: _____

   Third: _____   Answer: _____

2. Tara bought a railroad car kit for $4.98 and some track for $6.42. The sales clerk added 5% sales tax to the cost of her purchases. What was her total bill? (Remember: 5% = 0.05.)

   First: _____   Second: _____

   Third: _____   Answer: _____

3. Marcos works at the hobby shop. He earns $5.40 per hour for the first 35 hours he works. He earns $8.10 for each hour beyond that. One week, he worked $43\frac{1}{2}$ hours. What did he earn?

   First: _____   Second: _____

   Third: _____   Fourth: _____

   Answer: _____

4. The hobby shop had a special 25% off sale on all kites. Maria bought 3 box kites and 1 tetra kite during the sale. How much did the kites cost before sales tax was added?

   First: _____   Second: _____

   Third: _____   Fourth: _____

   Answer: _____

Kites	
	Reg. Price
Box Style	$14.95
Tetra Style	$19.95
All Others	$ 9.95

SPECIAL: 25% off regular price!

Checking Estimates and Computations

Aim: To use estimation and computation checks to judge if an answer is reasonable and accurate

What You Need to Know

You check an answer to see if it is (1) reasonable and (2) accurate. To check your computations, do one of the following:

- Add or multiply "backwards" (switch the numbers).
- Subtract to check addition; add to check subtraction.
- Divide to check multiplication; multiply to check division.

What if a computation checks as accurate but the answer makes no sense? You may have labeled your answer with the wrong unit. Or, you may have used the wrong plan.

Think About It

How can an answer be wrong if the computation is accurate?

Read the Examples. Notice how the computations are checked.

Example A Rudy, Tom, and Bev ran for class president. Rudy got 135 votes; Tom got 171 votes; Bev got 212 votes. How many votes were cast in the election?

Estimation:		**Computation:**	
	100		135
	200		171
	+ 200		+ 212
	500		518

Estimated Answer:	**Computed Answer:**
500 votes	518 votes

Computation Check: $212 + 171 + 135 = 518$

Example B Bev's friends worked from 3:10 P.M. until 6:05 P.M. making election posters. How long did they work?

Estimation:		**Computation:**	
	6		6 hr. 5 min.
	− 3		− 3 hr. 10 min.
	3		2 hr. 55 min.

Estimated Answer:	**Computed Answer:**
3 hours	2 hr. 55 min.

Computation Check:

$$2 \text{ hr. } 55 \text{ min.}$$
$$+ \ 3 \text{ hr. } 10 \text{ min.}$$
$$5 \text{ hr. } 65 \text{ min., or } 6 \text{ hr. } 5 \text{ min.}$$

In Example A, you add the votes in a different order to check your addition. In Example B, you add 3 hours and 10 minutes to your answer to check your subtraction.

Practice

Follow all five steps to solve each word problem below. Then write the estimated answer and the computed answer. Show your computation check in the box next to each word problem.

Morris School Enrollment	
6th Graders	547
7th Graders	582
8th Graders	683

1. If 518 eighth-graders voted in the class election, how many eighth-graders did not vote?

    Estimated Answer: _____   Computed Answer: _____

    1. Computation Check

2. The seventh-grade class elections will be held next week. If $\frac{5}{6}$ of the seventh-graders vote in the election, how many seventh-graders will vote?

    Estimated Answer: _____   Computed Answer: _____

    2. Computation Check

3. Rudy's friends made 23 election posters. They hung the same number of posters in 6 different classrooms. The extra posters were hung in the library. How many posters did they hang in each classroom?

    Estimated Answer: _____   Computed Answer: _____

    3. Computation Check

4. Juan, Claire, and Sue ran for eighth-grade class secretary. Juan received 186 votes. Claire and Sue each received the same number of votes as each other. If 518 students voted for class secretary, how many votes did Claire receive?

    Estimated Answer: _____   Computed Answer: _____

    4. Computation Check

5. The new class officers are planning a party for the whole school. They expect that $\frac{2}{3}$ of the students will attend the party. How many students do they expect to attend the party?

    Estimated Answer: _____   Computed Answer: _____

    5. Computation Check

Additional word problems for Lesson 15 skills practice are on page 97.

Unit 2 Review

A. On each line, write **T** or **F** to tell whether the statement is true or false.

_____ 1. Problems in daily life always have just the right amount of information.

_____ 2. When you need to find facts on a map, it is important first to study the whole map.

_____ 3. A table helps to organize all the numbers on a bus, train, or airline schedule.

_____ 4. You should read the title and all the labels on a graph before you begin to look for a specific fact.

_____ 5. Facts needed to solve a problem are always found somewhere on the problem page.

_____ 6. Routine word problems can be solved by adding, subtracting, multiplying, or dividing.

_____ 7. To join equal groups to find a total, the correct operation is subtraction.

_____ 8. When solving two-operation problems, you follow the same five steps— but you follow them twice.

_____ 9. Multiple-step problems may have two or more "hidden" questions to answer.

_____ 10. When checking your answer, if your computation is accurate, then your answer must be correct.

B. On each line, write the word that best completes the sentence.

_____ 11. To solve a word problem, you must have all the needed ____.

_____ 12. A type of graph that can be used to show change over time is a ____ graph.

_____ 13. To choose the correct ____ in a routine problem, visualize the action.

_____ 14. The answer to a hidden question becomes a fact needed for answering the ____ question.

_____ 15. To check addition or multiplication computations, you can add or multiply ____ (switch the numbers).

C. Circle the letter of the correct answer.

16. After dinner, Kris spent $\frac{1}{2}$ hour doing his math homework, $1\frac{1}{2}$ hours watching TV, and $1\frac{1}{4}$ hours doing his science homework. How much time did he spend doing homework?

    a. $1\frac{3}{4}$ hours   **b.** $3\frac{1}{4}$ hours   **c.** 2 hours   **d.** $1\frac{2}{6}$ hours

17. Doug drove from Hartford through Norwich and New London to Newport. How many miles did he drive?

    a. 116 miles   **c.** 102 miles

    b. 92 miles   **d.** 114 miles

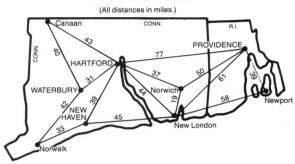

Driving Distances between Connecticut and Rhode Island

(All distances in miles.)

18. Sue took the 8:05 P.M. train from Boswell to Woodland Station. How long was her train ride?

    a. 58 min.   **c.** 1 hr. 3 min.

    b. 48 min.   **d.** 52 min.

Train Schedule

	Departs		Arrives Woodland Station
Tyler	Boswell	Spring	
6:10 A.M.	6:25 A.M.	6:35 A.M.	7:07 A.M.
8:30 A.M.	8:45 A.M.	8:55 A.M.	9:27 A.M.
5:25 P. M.	5:40 P. M.	5:50 P. M.	6:22 P. M.
7:50 P. M.	8:05 P. M.	8:35 P. M.	8:53 P. M.

19. How many more students were absent on Thursday than on Tuesday?

    a. 13 students   **c.** 14 students

    b. 12 students   **d.** 15 students

20. A large paper clip has a mass of 4 grams. A box of these clips has a mass of 1 kilogram. How many clips are in the box?

    a. 25 clips   **c.** 4,000 clips

    b. 4 clips   **d.** 250 clips

21. There are 23 rows of seats in the theater. Each row has 38 seats. How many people can be seated in the theater?

    a. 61 people   **c.** 854 people

    b. 874 people   **d.** 774 people

Students Absent

22. A slice of whole wheat bread has 55 calories. A slice of roast turkey has 100 calories. Adam used two slices of whole wheat bread and 1 slice of turkey to make a sandwich. How many calories were in his sandwich?

    a. 310 calories   **b.** 155 calories   **c.** 210 calories   **d.** 255 calories

23. Sheri bought 4 markers and 3 notebooks. Her total bill was $6.35. Each notebook cost $1.25. What was the price of each marker?

    a. $1.28   **b.** $0.65   **c.** $2.60   **d.** $0.85

D. Read and reread each word problem. Then follow the directions to show your solution to the problem.

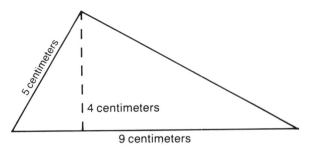

5 centimeters

4 centimeters

9 centimeters

24. Find the area of the triangle shown.
   a. Underline the question.
   b. Circle the needed facts in the problem.

   c. Describe your plan: _____

   _____

   d. If an estimate can be made, show it here: _____

   e. Carry out your plan. Answer: _____

   f. Check your answer. If you got an incorrect answer, tell how you know it is wrong. Then write the correct answer.

   _____

   _____

25. Megan had 43 photos of the class party and 21 photos of the class field trip. Suppose she puts 4 pictures on each page in her photo album. How many pages does she use?
   a. Underline the question.
   b. Circle the needed facts in the problem.

   c. Describe your plan: _____

   _____

   d. If an estimate can be made, show it here: _____

   e. Carry out your plan. Answer: _____

   f. Check your answer. If you got an incorrect answer, tell how you know it is wrong. Then write the correct answer.

   _____

   _____

Unit *Three*

MORE HELP WITH STRATEGIES

Lesson 16

Making a Diagram

Aim: To solve problems by drawing simple line diagrams

What You Need to Know

 If you have a problem you are not sure how to solve, begin by making a diagram of it. Then reread the problem. Ask yourself, "Is my drawing accurate? Have I included all the facts I can?" Then use the diagram and any other facts in the problem to decide on your plan for solving the problem.

Think About It

Why does it help to draw a diagram of a problem?

Read each problem below. Notice how each diagram helps.

Example A Julie watched a worker ant in an ant farm. The ant started at the surface. It dug straight down 1.5 cm and went back up. Then it went straight down the same tunnel for 3 cm and returned to the surface. On the third trip, it went straight down 4.5 cm and rested. How far did the ant travel in all?

Make a Diagram: **Answer:** *13.5 cm*

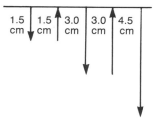

Example B The ant farm is 40 cm wide and 30 cm high. One worker ant walked all around the outside edge of the farm. It stopped to rest every 10 cm. How many times did the ant stop to rest during its trip around the farm?

Make a Diagram: **Answer:** *14 times*

In Example A, notice the arrows in the diagram. They show the distances and the directions the ant walked. Add 1.5 + 1.5 + 3 + 3 + 4.5. Example B shows each point around the farm where the ant stopped to rest. Count the points.

Practice

For each problem, make a diagram in the space provided. Write the answer. (Remember to check your answer for sense.)

1. At the science fair, all the electricity experiments are placed on one large square table. To make the large table, 9 smaller tables were pushed together. Each small square table is $1\frac{1}{2}$ yards on a side. What is the perimeter of the larger square? (Hint: *Perimeter* means "distance around.")

    Answer: _____

1. Diagram

2. Glenn has six different-colored dyes. The colors are red, blue, yellow, green, orange, and purple. He wants to mix 1 cup of each dye with 1 cup of every other dye to form new colors. How many new colors will he make?

    Answer: _____

2. Diagram

3. Beth is experimenting with solutions in test tubes. In each test tube, she places either water or alcohol. To each liquid, she adds salt or sugar. She then heats or cools each mixture. How many test tubes does Beth need to test all possible combinations? (Hint: Remember the branching "tree diagram" from Book 1.)

    Answer: _____

3. Diagram

4. Write a word problem of your own. Write a problem that making a diagram would help you to solve.

    _____

    _____

    _____

Making a Line Graph

Aim: To solve problems that involve constant speed or rate of change by making line graphs

<table>
<tr><td>

To solve a problem by making a graph:

1) Make a table.

2) Put the data from the problem in the table.

3) Find the pattern in the data.

4) Extend the table to 3 pairs of numbers.

5) Make the graph using the extended data.

</td></tr>
</table>

What You Need to Know

 A **line graph** is a special type of diagram. It helps you to "see" the data in a problem. Use a line graph in order to—

- **find unknown values that fall "in between" known values.** Suppose a car is traveling at a constant speed of 37 miles per hour. A line graph of this will tell you *how far* the car will travel in *any* amount of time.
- **compare similar events.** Suppose a fast-moving train starts traveling 1 minute after a slow-moving train. When will the faster train overtake the slower train? Make line graphs for both trains on the same grid. The trains will meet where the two lines cross.

Think About It

In the Example, what are the labels in the table and the graph?

_____

Study the Example. Notice how the table and graph are used.

Example A car moving at a constant speed travels 75 miles in 2 hours. How far will the car travel in 6 hours?

Make a table (label, extend):

Time (number of hours)	1	2	3
Distance (in miles)	37.5	75	112.5

Make a graph (label, plot points, draw line):

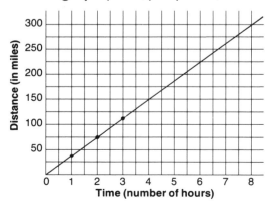

Answer (read the graph): *225 miles*

In the Example, you "read up" from 6 hours to where the grid line crosses the graphed line. Then "read left" to find that the car has traveled 225 miles. Suppose you wanted to find out how long it would take the car to travel 300 miles. How would you read the graph?

Practice

For each problem, first make a table with three pairs of numbers. Then make a graph by plotting points and drawing a line.

1. Maria is saving to buy a $180 typewriter. She saves the same amount each week. After 3 weeks she has saved $60. How long will it take her to save enough to buy the typewriter?

Make a table:

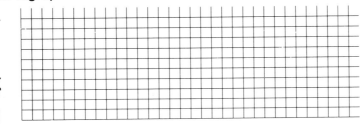

Make a graph: Answer: _____

Time (number of weeks)

2. How much money will Maria have saved in 7 weeks? _____

3. Ron started working at 9 A.M. and makes $6 per hour. Jay started working at 10 A.M. and makes $8 per hour. At what time will they both have made the same amount of money?

Table for Ron: _____

Table for Jay: _____

Make a graph for both   Answer: _____
boys on the same grid:

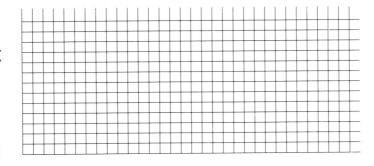

Time

4. How much will each boy earn by noon? _____

Writing an Equation

Aim: To solve problems by writing equations using one or more of the four operations

What You Need to Know

You can use equations to solve many word problems. Numbers, letters, and symbols stand for information in the problems. A letter, called a **variable**, stands for an unknown number.

You need to think about the "actions" in problems. This will help you decide which operations to use. Remember:

- **Add** to join different-sized groups.
- **Multiply** to join same-sized groups.
- **Subtract** to find how many are left or to compare amounts.
- **Divide** to break a group down into smaller, equal groups.

Often, more than one equation can be used. For instance, each of these could be used to describe the same situation:

$n + 3 = 7$ $3 + n = 7$ $7 - n = 3$ $7 - 3 = n$

Think About It

Why should you think about the action in a problem?

Read each problem. Notice how the variable is described. The equation is written *after* you think about the problem in phrases.

Example A Marty spent 15 hours building a patio for the Lovells. He charged them $1,200 for the patio. The materials cost $897.25. What was Marty's profit?

Variable: *Let* n = *Marty's profit*
Think: *price charged − cost of materials = profit*
Equation: *1,200 − 897.25 =* n   **Answer:** *$302.75*

Example B Mrs. Lovell budgeted $45 to buy bushes to go around her patio. Bushes are on sale for $5.75. How many can Mrs. Lovell buy and still stay within budget?

Variable: *Let* n = *number of bushes budgeted for*
Think: *money budgeted ÷ price per bush = bushes budgeted for*
Equation: *45.00 ÷ 5.75 =* n
Answer: *7 bushes (budgeted for 7.83 bushes)*

In Example A, the action could suggest either subtraction or addition. A subtraction equation is used. You could also use the addition equation $897.25 + n = 1{,}200$ (cost of materials + profit = amount charged). In Example B, the answer to the equation is not the final answer. Reread the question! The number of bushes Mrs. Lovell can *buy* is 7.

Practice

For each problem, describe the variable. Think about the action in the problem. Then write the equation and the answer. (Don't forget to follow all five problem solving steps!)

1. Mrs. Lovell drew this diagram of her new patio. What is the perimeter of the patio? (Do you need to look up *perimeter* in the Appendix?)

   Variable: Let $P =$ _____

   Equation: _____ Answer: _____

$9\frac{3}{4}$ ft.

$12\frac{1}{2}$ ft.

2. Marty put new baseboard molding in 2 bedrooms. He used 63 feet of molding for 1 bedroom. This is $1\frac{1}{2}$ times as much molding as he used in the second bedroom. How much molding did he use in the second bedroom?

   Variable: Let $n =$ _____

   Equation: _____ Answer: _____

3. Marty is replacing 4 windows and screens in the Snyder house. Each window costs $59. Each screen is an additional $4.95. How much will it cost for the 4 new windows and screens?

   Variable: Let $n =$ _____

   Equation: _____ Answer: _____

4. Jill drew this diagram of her backyard. Marty is putting in a new fence along the back and one side. Fencing comes in 6-foot sections. How many sections of fencing should Marty buy?

   Variable: Let $n =$ _____

   Equation: _____ Answer: _____

Jill's house

47 ft.

22.5 ft.

5. Write a word problem of your own. Write a problem that can be solved with an equation.

   _____

   _____

   _____

Additional word problems for Lesson 18 skills practice are on page 100.

45

Using a Formula

Aim: To solve problems using rate formulas

What You Need to Know

A **formula** is a special kind of equation. It is useful for solving certain types of problems. These are problems that have the same basic situation. The numbers are all that change. Review some common formulas on Appendix page 121.

In this lesson, you will use two formulas that contain the variable r to stand for "rate." The word *rate* means a measured change. It is "something per something," as in miles per hour or percent per year.

$d = rt$ (distance = rate × time)

$i = prt$ (interest = principal × rate × time)

The formula $d = rt$ solves certain kinds of **motion** problems. The distance, the rate, *or* the time is unknown. The formula $i = prt$ is used to compute **simple interest**. In a word problem for this formula, *one* of the following is unknown:

- Interest (i) is the amount paid for the use of money.
- Principal (p) is the amount borrowed or invested.
- Rate (r) is the percent at which interest is charged or earned per year.
- Time (t) is the number of years for which the money is borrowed or invested.

Think About It

What words do the letters in the interest formula ($i = prt$) stand for?

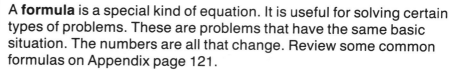

Read each problem. Notice how letters are replaced by numbers.

Example A A runner ran a distance of 26 miles in $2\frac{1}{2}$ hours. What was the runner's average rate of speed?

The Formula: $d = rt$

Replace the letters you know: $26 = r \times 2\frac{1}{2}$

Answer: *10.4 miles per hour*

Example B Irene borrowed $1,800 at an interest rate of 9.5% for 6 months. How much interest did she pay on her loan?

The Formula: $i = prt$

Replace the letters you know: $i = 1,800 \times .095 \times .5$

Answer: *$85.50*

In Example A, the formula $d = rt$ is used to find the runner's average rate of speed. The distance is in miles and the time is in hours. So, the rate is shown as miles per hour.

In Example B, the formula $i = prt$ is used. Notice that the percent is written as a decimal (9.5% = 0.095). The time is in years (6 months = 0.5 year). When you use this formula, always change the percent to a decimal. Always show the time in years.

Practice

Use the formula $d = rt$ or $i = prt$ to solve each problem.

1. A car is moving at a rate of 50 miles per hour. How long will it take the car to travel 625 miles?

    The formula: _____   Replace letters: _____

    Answer: _____

2. Casey invested $1,000 at 5% simple interest for $3\frac{1}{2}$ years. How much interest did he earn?

    The formula: _____   Replace letters: _____

    Answer: _____

3. An airplane travels a distance of 3,025 miles in 5 hours 30 minutes. At what rate of speed is the airplane traveling?

    The formula: _____   Replace letters: _____

    Answer: _____

4. Rosita invested $850 for 2 years at simple interest. After 2 years, she had earned $119. What was the interest rate?

    The formula: _____   Replace letters: _____

    Answer: _____

5. Jake borrowed $1,500 at 12.5% interest. For how long did he borrow the money if the interest he paid was $562.50?

    The formula: _____   Replace letters: _____

    Answer: _____

6. Write a word problem of your own. Write a problem that you could use one of the rate formulas to solve.

    _____

    _____

    _____

Lesson 20

Solving a Simpler Problem

Aim: To use simpler problem situations to find the patterns that will solve the complex problems

What You Need to Know

A problem with hard numbers or with a complex situation can seem harder than it really is. Leave it for a moment. Think of a similar but simpler problem. How would you solve it? Then apply the same plan to the original problem. Sometimes, you will need to solve several simpler problems in order to find a *pattern* in how the answers are found. You will learn more about that in this lesson.

Think About It

What can make word problems seem hard to solve?

Read each problem. Notice how the situation is made simpler.

Example A How many triangles are in this figure?

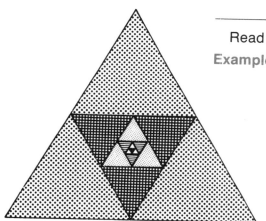

Simplify: *Look at the figure in stages starting from the inside and working out.*

1st stage	▼	1 triangle
2nd stage	◭	3 small + 1 larger = 4 triangles
3rd stage	◮	3 small + 1 larger = 4 triangles

Pattern: *Each stage after the first adds 4 new triangles.*
Answer: *21 triangles (1 + 4 + 4 + 4 + 4 + 4 = 21)*

Example B There are 18 members in the chess club. If each member plays one chess game with every other member, how many chess games will be played?

Simplify: *Think about the number of games if there were 2, 3, or 4 members in the club.*

② members	AB → 1		1 game
③ members	AB BC AC → 2 + 1		3 games
④ members	AB BC CD AC BD AD → 3 + 2 + 1		6 games

Pattern: *The number of games is the sum of the numbers from 1-less-than-the-number-of-members down to 1.*
Answer: *153 chess games (17 + 16 + 15 + ... + 1)*

In Example A, simplify the problem by looking at each stage of the figure. The first, innermost piece is one small triangle. Each stage after that adds 4 new triangles. There are five 4-triangle stages. There are, therefore, 21 triangles in all.

Example B is simplified by thinking about a club with 2, 3, or 4 members. That establishes the pattern for finding the number of games for any number of members. Then apply that pattern to 18 members.

Practice

For each problem, think of similar but simpler problems. Explain the pattern. Then use it to solve the original problem.

1. How many triangles are in this figure?

   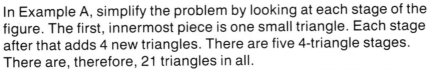

   Pattern: _____

   _____

   _____ Answer: _____

2. There are 15 students who have signed up to play in the annual handball tournament. If each student plays every other student, how many games will be played? (Hint: Look again at Example B.)

   Pattern: _____

   _____

   _____ Answer: _____

3. Terri has 15 small, square tables. She plans to use the tables for a party. Each table can seat one person on a side. If all the tables are pushed together to make one long table, how many people can sit at that table?

   Pattern: _____

   _____

   _____ Answer: _____

4. How many squares are in a checkerboard? The squares can be different sizes and they can overlap. (Hint: Think about the number of squares in a 1 × 1 square, a 2 × 2 square, and a 3 x 3 square.)

   Pattern: _____

   _____

   _____ Answer: _____

Lesson 21

Using Ratio Proportions

Aim: To solve problems using ratio proportions

What You Need to Know

A **ratio** is a way to compare numbers. A ratio can be shown as a fraction. Suppose that you drink 3 cups of milk with every 2 muffins you eat. The ratio of cups of milk to muffins is 3 to 2. Shown as a fraction, this ratio is $\frac{3}{2}$. Ratios can be used to solve problems that involve rates or comparisons.

A **proportion** is an equation that states that two ratios are equal. A proportion is true if the *cross products* are equal.

Cross Products

$2 \times 6 = 12$
$3 \times 4 = 12$

Therefore, $\frac{3}{2} = \frac{6}{4}$ is a proportion.

If you know any three numbers in a proportion, you can find the fourth number. Use cross products to write an equation.

Think About It

A proportion is an _____ stating that two

_____ are equal.

Read each problem. Notice how the proportion is set up and solved in each.

Example A   Sean's recipe for waffles calls for 1.5 cups of flour for every 2 eggs. If Sean uses 6 cups of flour, how many eggs should he use?

The Proportion: $\frac{1.5}{2} \diagdown \frac{6}{n}$ $\dfrac{\text{cups of flour}}{\text{number of eggs}}$

The Cross Products: $1.5n = 12; n = 12 \div 1.5; n = 8$
Answer: *8 eggs*

Example B   This is a scale drawing of Beth's apartment. The scale is written below the drawing. Use the drawing and the scale to find the real width of Beth's kitchen. (Hint: First measure the width of the kitchen on the scale drawing.)

The Proportion: $\frac{2}{3} \diagdown \frac{2}{n}$ $\dfrac{\text{length on drawing (in cm)}}{\text{actual length (in m)}}$

The Cross Products: $2n = 6; n = 3$
Answer: *3 meters*

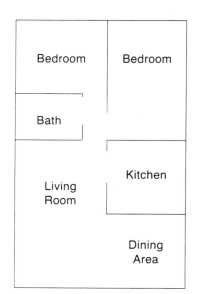

Scale: 2 cm = 3 m

In Example A, read the proportion as "1.5 cups of flour is to 2 eggs as 6 cups of flour is to *n* eggs." Use the cross products to write an equation to solve for the unknown (*n* eggs). Example B shows how to use equal ratios to solve problems involving scale drawings.

Practice

For each problem, write the proportion in the box. Then write the cross products and the answer. Use the scale drawing on page 50 for items 1 and 2.

1. What is the actual length of Beth's living room?

   Cross Products: _____ Answer: _____

   1. The Proportion

2. Beth wants to add onto her house a garage that is 7.5 meters wide. She will use the same scale as was used for her house. How wide will the garage be in her scale drawing?

   Cross Products: _____ Answer: _____

   2. The Proportion

3. Alex is making spaghetti sauce for a school fund-raising dinner. He needs 2 cups of sauce for every 5 people. He wants to make enough sauce for 240 people. How many *gallons* of sauce should he make? (Hint: First find how many cups of sauce he needs. Then convert cups to gallons.)

   Cross Products: _____ Answer: _____

   3. The Proportion

4. Alex's recipe calls for 5 onions for every 3 pounds of meat. If he uses 42 pounds of meat, how many onions will he need?

   Cross Products: _____ Answer: _____

   4. The Proportion

5. Lucia drives 140 miles in 3.5 hours. At this rate, how far will she drive in 6.5 hours?

   Cross Products: _____ Answer: _____

   5. The Proportion

6. Write a word problem of your own. Write a problem that using a proportion (equal ratios) would help to solve.

   _____

   _____

Lesson 22

Using Logical Reasoning

Aim: To solve problems by using deductive logic

What You Need to Know

Logical reasoning is a way to solve "puzzle" problems. Puzzle problems have many *possible* answers. There are clues in the problems. You need to use logical reasoning, or **deductive logic,** as you read the clues. Then you can rule out or approve each possible answer.

A table or chart can be used to organize the facts in a puzzle problem. As you read the clues, mark the outcomes in the table. These problems will differ from others you have done. They often do not include numbers.

Think About It

Why is a table helpful when you use logic to solve a problem?

Read the Example. Notice how the table is set up and marked.

Example Ann, Barb, and Sara each get to school a different way. One rides a bus, one roller-skates, and one walks. Use the clues to find out how each girl gets to school.

Clue 1: Barb and the walker eat lunch together.

Clue 2: The bus rider swims on Ann's team.

Clue 3: Sara roller-skates to school.

Set Up a Table: Mark the table for each clue. Use X to rule out a choice. Use ✔ to approve a choice.

After Clue 1: You know Barb is NOT the walker. Place an X in Barb's column across from "Walk."

After Clue 2: You know Ann is NOT the bus rider. Put an X in Ann's column across from "Bus."

After Clue 3: You know Sara is the roller skater. Put a ✔ in Sara's column across from "Skates."

Solve the Puzzle: From what you have marked on the table, you can solve the puzzle.

- Since Sara is the roller skater, she cannot be the walker or the bus rider. Put X's there.
- There is only one choice left for the bus rider — Barb. Complete her column.
- Ann must be the walker!

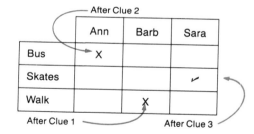

	Ann	Barb	Sara
Bus	X		
Skates			✔
Walk		X	

After Clue 2

After Clue 1

After Clue 3

In the Example, the clues are considered one at a time. The table is marked with an X (to rule out a possible solution) or with a ✔ (to approve a possible solution). After all the clues are marked, the table is studied to solve the puzzle.

Practice

For each item 1–4, first set up a table on a separate sheet of paper. Mark your table for each clue. After you solve the problem, be sure to check your answer against the clues. Then write your answer here.

1. Dan, Lisa, and Amy have different occupations. They work as an accountant, a baker, and a carpenter. Use the clues to find each person's occupation.
   Clue 1: Dan and the accountant play tennis together.
   Clue 2: The carpenter helped Amy build a garage.
   Clue 3: Lisa's bakery shop is open six days a week.

   Answer: _____

2. Ray, Sue, and Carlos each read a book about their favorite sport. The books were about swimming, soccer, and tennis. Use the clues to find what Carlos's book was about.
   Clue 1: One of Sue's friends likes swimming.
   Clue 2: Ray likes to swim.
   Clue 3: The one who likes tennis asked Carlos to play a game.

   Answer: _____

3. Fawn, Fern, and Felix are movie-goers. One likes monster movies, one likes romantic movies, and one likes space movies. The one who likes monster movies lives next door to Fern. The ones who like romantic and monster movies helped Felix to find his lost homework. Who likes which kind of movies?

   Answer: _____

4. Jason, Jacob, Joel, and James each own a different pet. They have a dog, a cat, a hamster, and a rabbit. Jason has the smallest pet. The dog and cat owners both took care of Joel's pet when he went on vacation. Jacob's dog likes to chase the cat up a tree. What kind of pet does James own?

   Answer: _____

5. Write a word problem of your own. Write a problem that using logical reasoning would help you to solve.

   _____

   _____

Exact or Estimated Answers

Aim: To decide which problems can be solved by finding estimated rather than exact answers

What You Need to Know

You use estimated numbers as often as exact numbers in your daily life. You estimate when an exact answer is *not possible*. (How many people will be born in the U.S. next year? How many fish are in a lake?) You also estimate when an exact number is *not needed*. (About how much time do you spend studying each week? Do you have enough money to buy a taco for lunch?)

Before you decide on a plan for solving a word problem, ask yourself, "Do I need an exact answer? Or, is an estimated answer enough?" If an estimated answer is enough, you may be able to do the work mentally.

Think About It

When can you use an estimated answer to solve a problem?

Read each problem. Notice whether an exact or estimated answer is used to solve the problem.

Example A Yoko has saved $40 to buy new school clothes. She wants to buy a skirt for $18.95, a sweater for $11.25, and a belt for $3.95. Does she have enough money?

Exact or Estimated? *Estimated*

The Execution: *Think: 20 + 10 + 4 = 34*

The Answer: *Yes, Yoko has enough money.*

Example B The tax on the three items Yoko bought in Example A was $1.71. Yoko wants to pay for these 3 items by check. For how much should she write the check?

Exact or Estimated? *Exact*

The Execution: *18.95*   **Answer:** *$35.86*
11.25
3.95
1.71
35.86

In Example A, an estimated answer is enough. It is not necessary to know the exact cost of the items. All you need to know is that the total cost is not over $40. In Example B, an exact amount must be written on the check.

Practice

For each problem, first state whether an exact or estimated answer is necessary. Then solve the problem.

1. The owner of the store wants to keep at least 500 sweaters in stock at all times. She has sweaters on 3 racks. There are 185 sweaters on the first rack, 219 sweaters on the second rack, and 179 sweaters on the third rack. Does she need more sweaters in stock?

   Exact or Estimated? _____   Answer: _____

2. Kyle bought two pairs of shoes during the BUY ONE—GET ONE HALF PRICE shoe sale. One pair cost $19.96. The other pair cost $23.95. How much did the two pairs of shoes cost before tax was added?

   Exact or Estimated? _____   Answer: _____

3. Liz works in the store on Mondays, Wednesdays and Fridays. Last week she worked 7 hours 50 minutes on Monday, 6 hours 15 minutes on Wednesday, and 8 hours 45 minutes on Friday. About how many hours did Liz work last week?

   Exact or Estimated? _____   Answer: _____

4. Pam has $50. Can she buy a jacket for $27.95, two pairs of socks for $3.15 each, and a shirt for $11.95?

   Exact or Estimated? _____   Answer: _____

5. Will and Scott went shopping together. Will's bill was $39.95. He gave the clerk a 50-dollar bill. Scott's bill was $7.95. He gave the clerk a 20-dollar bill. Who received more change back from the clerk?

   Exact or Estimated? _____   Answer: _____

6. Write a word problem of your own. Write a problem in which an estimated answer will be enough to solve the problem.

   _____

   _____

   _____

Shoe Sale
Buy One—Get One Half Price
Buy one pair of shoes, get the second pair of equal or lesser value for half price.

More Than One Strategy

Aim: To recognize that there is often more than one way to solve a word problem

What You Need to Know

You have learned many strategies for solving word problems. Often, as soon as you read a problem, you will know which strategy to use. For routine problems, you simply add, subtract, multiply, or divide. For other problems, you may not be as sure what to do. If you try one strategy and it does not lead to a correct answer, reread the problem. Then try another strategy. Any strategy that gives you the correct answer is right for you!

Think About It

If you choose a strategy that doesn't work, what should you do?

Read each problem below. Notice the two strategies that are suggested for solving each.

Example A Ian is making lemonade. He needs 2 lemons for every 3 cups of water. How many cups of water should Ian put with the juice from 10 lemons?

Strategies:

Make a table.   or   *Use a ratio proportion.*

Lemons	2	4	6	8	10
Cups water	3	6	9	12	15

$\dfrac{2}{3} = \dfrac{10}{n}$ $2n = 30;$ $n = 15$

Answer: *15 cups of water*

Example B Sue walks $4\frac{1}{2}$ blocks to school. She started walking toward school and then remembered her homework. She walked back home for her homework and then walked to school. If she walked 6 blocks in all, how far had Sue walked before she remembered her homework?

Strategies:

Draw a diagram.   or   *Write an equation.*

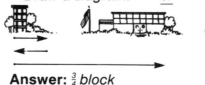

$n + n + 4\frac{1}{2} = 6$
$2n + 4\frac{1}{2} = 6$
$2n = 1\frac{1}{2}$
$n = \frac{3}{4}$

Answer: $\frac{3}{4}$ *block*

Making a table and using a ratio proportion are two strategies for Example A. You could also solve that problem by making a graph! Example B is solved by drawing a diagram or by writing an equation. You might even use both strategies. The picture makes it easier to see the action. That makes it easier to choose the correct operation for the equation.

Practice

Read each word problem. Choose a strategy to solve the problem. Then use your strategy to answer the question. Be sure to follow all five problem-solving steps.

1. Andy is putting 1-foot square tiles in his hallway. The hallway is 4 feet by 14 feet. The tile comes in boxes of 12 tiles each. How many boxes of tiles does he need to buy?

   Strategy: _____ Answer: _____

2. A bus is traveling at a rate of 40 miles per hour. How long will it take the bus to travel 380 miles?

   Strategy: _____ Answer: _____

3. Juanita used 22 feet of fencing to make a triangular pen for her pet. One side of the pen is $10\frac{1}{2}$ feet. Another side is $5\frac{1}{4}$ feet. How long is the third side?

   Strategy: _____ Answer: _____

4. A 3-pound bag of apples costs $2.07. How much should you pay for 10 pounds of apples?

   Strategy: _____ Answer: _____

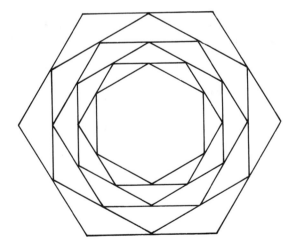

5. How many triangles are in this picture?

   Strategy: _____ Answer: _____

Additional word problems for **Lesson 24** skills practice are on page 106.

Unit 3 Review

A. On each line, write **T** or **F** to tell whether the statement is true or false.

_____ 1. If you have a problem that you are not sure how to solve, it may help to draw a diagram.

_____ 2. After you make a line graph to solve a problem, you should make a table for the facts in the problem.

_____ 3. Thinking about the actions in problems will help you to decide which operations to use.

_____ 4. Only one correct equation can be used to solve a problem.

_____ 5. If the numbers or situation make a problem seem difficult, it often helps to think of a similar but simpler problem.

_____ 6. A proportion is true if the cross products are equal.

_____ 7. "Puzzle" problems can usually be solved by adding or subtracting.

_____ 8. A table often helps to organize the facts in a puzzle problem.

_____ 9. You rarely need to find an exact answer to a word problem.

_____ 10. As soon as you read a word problem, you will know the best strategy for solving it.

B. On each line, write the word that best completes the sentence.

_____ 11. If you want to find an unknown value that falls in between known values, or if you want to compare similar events, you can use a _____ graph.

_____ 12. In an equation, a letter that can stand for different values is called a _____.

_____ 13. In the formula $i = prt,$ the letter i stands for _____.

_____ 14. An equation that states that two ratios are equal is called a _____.

_____ 15. When an exact answer to a problem is either not possible or not needed, you use an _____ answer.

C. Circle the letter of the correct answer.

16. Suppose 5 people are meeting each other. If each person shakes hands with every other person once, how many handshakes will there be?

    a. 8 handshakes   **b.** 20 handshakes   **c.** 10 handshakes   **d.** 15 handshakes

17. A train traveling at a constant speed travels 150 miles in 4 hours. How far will the train travel in 6 hours?

    a. 37.5 miles   **b.** 225 miles   **c.** 900 miles   **d.** 450 miles

18. Jay worked 30 hours last week. That was $6\frac{1}{2}$ hours more than Jean worked. How many hours did Jean work?

    a. $24\frac{1}{2}$ hours   **b.** $36\frac{1}{2}$ hours   **c.** 13 hours   **d.** $23\frac{1}{2}$ hours

19. Pat has 3 times as many coins as Sue has. Sue has 15 coins. How many coins does Pat have?

    a. 45 coins   **b.** 5 coins   **c.** 18 coins   **d.** 12 coins

20. A bus is traveling at a rate of 40 miles per hour. How long will it take the bus to travel 100 miles?

    a. 140 minutes   **b.** 60 minutes   **c.** $2\frac{1}{2}$ hours   **d.** 2 hours

21. Josh invested $100 at 6% simple interest for 5 years. How much interest did he earn?

    a. $20   **b.** $50   **c.** $30   **d.** $60

22. Raul has 12 small square tables. Each table can seat only one person on a side. Suppose the tables are pushed together to make one long table. How many people can sit at that long table?

    a. 48 people   **b.** 26 people   **c.** 24 people   **d.** 36 people

23. A map is drawn with a scale of 2 cm = 5 km. Suppose a road on the map measures 4 centimeters. How long is the actual road?

    a. 10 centimeters   **b.** 20 centimeters   **c.** 10 kilometers   **d.** 20 kilometers

24. These clues describe a number. What is the number?
    Clue 1: The number has 3 digits.
    Clue 2: The number is less than 200.
    Clue 3: The number can be divided evenly by 12 and by 9.
    Clue 4: The ones digit is less than the tens digit.

    a. 108   **b.** 216   **c.** 180   **d.** 132

25. Steve kept this record of the number of miles he jogged: Monday—$2\frac{1}{4}$ miles; Tuesday—$3\frac{3}{4}$ miles; Wednesday— $1\frac{1}{8}$ miles; Thursday—$3\frac{1}{4}$ miles; Friday—$2\frac{3}{4}$ miles. About how far did Steve jog in the 5 days?

    a. about 13 miles   **b.** about 17 miles   **c.** about 11 miles   **d.** about 15 miles

D. Read and reread each word problem. Then follow the directions to show your solution to the problem.

26. An airplane is traveling at an average speed of 550 miles per hour. About how far will the airplane travel in $3\frac{1}{2}$ hours?
    a. Underline the question.
    b. Circle the needed facts in the problem.

    c. Describe your plan: _____

    _____

    d. If an estimate can be made, show it here: _____

    e. Carry out your plan. Answer: _____

    f. Check your answer. If you got an incorrect answer, tell how you know it is wrong. Then write the correct answer.

    _____

    _____

27. There are 32 students in Mrs. Aplin's class. Suppose 3 out of 4 students walk to school. How many students in Mrs. Aplin's class walk to school?
    a. Underline the question.
    b. Circle the needed facts in the problem.

    c. Describe your plan: _____

    _____

    d. If an estimate can be made, show it here: _____

    e. Carry out your plan. Answer: _____

    f. Check your answer. If you got an incorrect answer, tell how you know it is wrong. Then write the correct answer.

    _____

    _____

Unit *Four*

REAL-LIFE
APPLICATIONS

Checking Accounts

Aim: To solve problems involving checking accounts

What You Need to Know

When you have money in a bank **checking account,** you write *checks* to use the money. A *check register* is used to keep a record of the checks you write (the money you take out) and the deposits you make (the money you put in). The register shows the **balance,** or the amount of money left in the account. Each time you write a check, you subtract. Each time you make a deposit, you add.

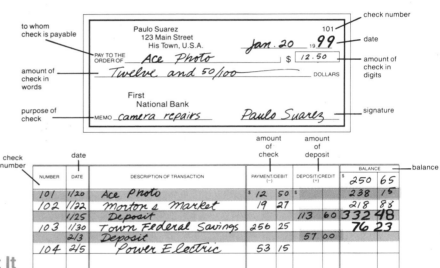

Think About It

After Paulo Suarez wrote check number 101, what was the balance

in his account? _____

Read the problems below. Notice where the facts are found.

Example A What was Paulo's balance after he made the deposit on January 25? Write the new balance on the register.

The Execution: 218.88   **Answer:** *$332.48*
                     + 113.60
                      332.48

Example B What was the balance after Paulo wrote check number 103? Write the new balance on the register.

The Execution: 332.48   **Answer:** *$76.23*
                     − 256.25
                      76.23

In Example A, Paulo is adding money to his checking account. So, you add to find the new balance. In Example B, you subtract to find the new balance. Paulo is using some of the money in his account to pay Town Federal Savings.

Practice

Answer these questions about checks and check registers.

1. May wrote a check for $27.35 on January 20, 1999. She made the check out to Bradley's Bookshop to pay for a dictionary. Complete May's check.

```
┌─────────────────────────────────────────────────────────────────┐
│                                                                   │
│   May Butler                                           101        │
│      456 Central Ave.                                             │
│        Her Town, U.S.A.           _____ 19 ____               │
│  PAY TO THE                                                       │
│  ORDER OF _____  $ ┌──────────┐       │
│                                                 └──────────┘       │
│  _____  DOLLARS        │
│                                                                   │
│     Continental Bank                                              │
│                                                                   │
│  MEMO _____        _____           │
│                                                                   │
└─────────────────────────────────────────────────────────────────┘
```

Use the check register on page 62 and the answers to Examples A and B to solve Practice items 2 and 3.

2. What was Paulo's balance after his deposit on February 3?

_____

3. What was Paulo's balance after his check to Power Electric?

_____

4. Janna had $413.60 in her checking account. On February 5, she wrote a check to The Sport Shop for $63.15. On February 7, she wrote a check to Fred's Garage for $125.20. How much money does Janna have left in her account after writing those 2 checks?

_____

5. This is Janna's check register. Complete the register for the checks Janna wrote in Practice item 4.

NUMBER	DATE	DESCRIPTION OF TRANSACTION	PAYMENT/DEBIT (−)	DEPOSIT/CREDIT (+)	BALANCE
					$ 413 60
			$	$	

Lesson 26

Unit Pricing

Aim: To solve problems by finding unit prices in order to determine "best buys"

What You Need to Know

To find the "best buy" when you shop, you can compare unit pricing. The unit price of an item can mean either:

- the price for one item, or
- the price for one unit of an item.

$$\text{unit price} = \frac{\text{total cost}}{\text{number of units}}$$

To find the best buy when shopping, use the above formula with each item. Compare the unit prices to find the best buy.

Think About It

How can finding unit prices help you to be a wise shopper?

_____

_____

Read the problems below. Notice how unit prices are found.

Example A A 12-ounce can of nuts sells for $1.74. What is the unit price?

Formula: $\textit{unit price} = \dfrac{\textit{total cost}}{\textit{number of units}}$

$= \dfrac{1.74}{12}$

$= .145 \ or \ .15 \ (rounded \ up)$

Answer: *$0.15 per ounce*

Example B Look at the ads for apples. Which store has the better buy on apples?

Find the unit prices:

At Buy-Rite Foods: $\dfrac{1.45}{2} = .725$, rounding to .73

At Food Fair: $\dfrac{2.07}{3} = .69$

Compare the unit prices: *$0.69 per pound is less than $0.73 per pound.*

Answer: *Food Fair has the better buy on apples.*

Buy-Rite Foods
Apples
2 lb. $1.45

Food Fair
Apples
3 lb. $2.07

In Example A, the unit is an ounce. The unit price tells you that 1 ounce of nuts costs $0.15 (rounded to the nearest cent). In Example B, you find the best buy by comparing the unit prices of apples at two food stores. The unit is a pound.

Practice

For items 1–4, find the unit price to the nearest cent.

1. 5 bars of soap for $3.80 _____

2. 32 ounces of apple sauce for $1.12: _____

3. 4-pack of orange juice for $1.18: _____

4. 1.5 pounds of cheese for $3.90: _____

For Practice items 5–8, find the unit prices of the items. Then tell which is the better buy. For item 8, you will need to do one *more* step in order to answer the question.

5. 5-lb. bag of onions for $1.60 <u>or</u> 8-lb. bag of onions for $2.68

   Unit price for 5 lb.: _____

   Unit price for 8 lb.: _____

   Better Buy: _____

6. package of 8 rolls for $1.60 <u>or</u> package of 12 rolls for $2.16

   Unit price for 8 rolls: _____

   Unit price for 12 rolls: _____

   Better Buy: _____

7. 20-oz. can of sliced pineapple for 78¢ <u>or</u> 7-oz. can for 35¢

   Unit price for 20-ounce can: _____

   Unit price for 7-ounce can: _____

   Better Buy: _____

8. Two cans of Juicy Orange juice sell for $2.49. Three cans of Tastee Orange juice sell for $3.99. You buy 12 cans at the better buy. How much do you spend?

   Unit price for Juicy Orange: _____

   Unit price for Tastee Orange: _____

   Better Buy: _____   Answer: _____

Additional word problems for Lesson 26 skills practice are on page 108.

Lesson 27

Recipes

Aim: To change quantities in recipes in order to make the needed number of servings

What You Need to Know

A **recipe** tells how much of each item, or *ingredient,* to use, such as "2 cups" or "3 teaspoons." A recipe tells how much of each ingredient to use to serve a certain number of people. Sometimes you need to feed more or fewer people. Here is how to change a recipe's serving size:

- First, decide on the number of servings you need. (Example: You want to serve 4 people.)
- Second, compare this number with the number of servings for the recipe. Show this as a ratio written as a fraction. (Example: The recipe serves 3 people. The ratio is $\frac{4}{3}$.)
- Third, multiply *each ingredient amount in the recipe* by the ratio ($\frac{4}{3}$). The new amounts are the measures to use.

Think About It

What do you compare when you write a ratio to change a recipe?

Notice how a ratio is used to solve each problem below.

Example A Read Sue's recipe for meat loaf. Sue wants to prepare a meat loaf dinner for 12 people. How much ground beef does she need?

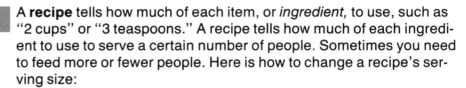

Sue's Meat Loaf	
1½ pounds ground beef	1 egg, beaten
1 cup bread crumbs	¼ cup minced onion
1¼ cups milk	½ teaspoon pepper

Mix all ingredients thoroughly. Spread in ungreased loaf pan 9" x 5" x 3". Bake in 350° oven for 1½ hours.

Serves 4

Ratio: $\frac{servings\ needed}{servings\ in\ recipe} = \frac{12}{4}$, or 3

The Execution: *needed amount = ratio × recipe amount*
needed amount ground beef $= 3 \times 1\frac{1}{2} = 4\frac{1}{2}$

Answer: $4\frac{1}{2}$ *pounds*

Example B How much onion is needed to make a meat loaf for 2 people?

Ratio: $\frac{servings\ needed}{servings\ in\ recipe} = \frac{2}{4} = \frac{1}{2}$

The Execution: *needed amount = ratio × recipe amount*
needed amount onions $= \frac{1}{2} \times \frac{1}{4} = \frac{1}{8}$

Answer: $\frac{1}{8}$ *cup*

In Example A, the ratio comparing the servings needed to the servings in the recipe is $\frac{12}{4}$, or 3. Sue wants to serve three times as many people as the recipe serves. She must triple the recipe. She must multiply the amount of each ingredient by 3.

In Example B, the ratio is $\frac{2}{4}$ or $\frac{1}{2}$. Sue wants to serve $\frac{1}{2}$ as many people as the recipe serves. She must multiply the amount of each ingredient by $\frac{1}{2}$.

Practice

Solve each problem using the facts in the recipes. Show the ratio and the answer.

1. What amount of bread crumbs would Sue need to make meat loaf for 6 people?

    Ratio: _____   Answer: _____

2. How much milk would Sue use to make meat loaf for 2 people?

    Ratio: _____   Answer: _____

Banana Oatmeal Muffins	
2 eggs	1 cup oats
$\frac{1}{2}$ cup cooking oil	$\frac{1}{4}$ cup wheat germ
1 cup mashed bananas	$\frac{3}{4}$ cup whole wheat flour
$\frac{3}{4}$ cup honey	1 teaspoon baking powder
	1 teaspoon baking soda
Sift together flour, baking powder, and baking soda. Set aside. Beat oil and eggs. Add bananas to egg mixture. Add honey and flour mixture, blending by hand. Stir in oats and wheat germ. Fill muffin cups $\frac{2}{3}$ full. Bake at 375° for 20 minutes.	
	Makes 18 muffins

3. How much whole wheat flour would you use to make 36 muffins?

    Ratio: _____   Answer: _____

4. How much wheat germ would you use to make 12 muffins?

    Ratio: _____   Answer: _____

5. Suppose you have only 1 egg. How many muffins can you make? (Hint: Compare eggs you have with eggs you need to form a ratio.)

    Ratio: _____   Answer: _____

Budgets

Aim: To solve problems about budgets by reading circle graphs

What You Need to Know

A **budget** is a plan for using money. It helps people or companies to use their money wisely. A **circle graph** can help you to "see" all parts of a budget. The graph makes it easy to compare the amounts of money to be spent in various areas.

The facts shown on a circle graph usually are shown in **percents.** The sum of all percents should be 100%. The greater the percent, the greater the region in the graph.

Think About It

Study the circle graph on this page. What is its title?

Gina's Budget

Read each problem. Notice where the information is found in the circle graph to help answer each question.

Example A   Gina has a part-time job at a grocery store. The circle graph shows how she decided to budget the money she earns. Last week Gina earned $84. How much money should she have put away as savings last week?

Needed Graph Facts: *25% for savings*

The Plan: Find *25% of $84.*

The Execution:

$$\begin{array}{r} 84 \\ \times\ .25 \\ \hline 420 \\ 168 \\ \hline 21.00 \end{array}$$

Answer: *$21*

Example B   This week Gina earned $72. She wants to buy a new jacket. The jacket costs $34.99. If she spends only the money she has budgeted for clothing this week, can she buy the jacket?

Needed Graph Facts: *30% for clothing*

The Plan: *Find 30% of 72.*

The Execution:

$$\begin{array}{r} 72 \\ \times\ .30 \\ \hline 21.60 \end{array}$$

Answer: *No, she cannot buy the jacket.*

In Example A, the needed fact in the graph is found in the region for "savings." Gina budgeted 25% of her earnings for savings. So, take 25% of $84 to find the amount of money budgeted to be saved for that week.

In Example B, the information in the graph is found in the region for "clothes." To answer the question, compare the amount budgeted for clothes ($21.60) to the cost of the jacket ($34.99).

Practice

For each problem, write the needed graph facts, the plan, and the answer. Use the circle graph on page 68 for items 1 and 2.

1. If Gina earns $92, how much can she spend on lunches?

    Needed Graph Facts: _____

    The Plan: _____ Answer: _____

2. In February, Gina earned $344. She wants to buy a new camera. The camera costs $75. Can Gina buy the camera with the money she budgeted for savings in February?

    Needed Graph Facts: _____

    The Plan: _____ Answer: _____

Mr. and Mrs. Simon's combined take-home pay is $48,000 a year. They made this graph to show how they plan to budget their money.

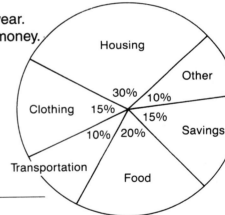

3. How much money have Mr. and Mrs. Simon budgeted for housing?

    Needed Graph Facts: _____

    The Plan: _____ Answer: _____

4. How much money have Mr. and Mrs. Simon budgeted for food and clothing together?

    Needed Graph Facts: _____

    The Plan: _____ Answer: _____

5. How much more money have Mr. and Mrs. Simon budgeted for savings than for transportation?

    Needed Graph Facts: _____

    The Plan: _____ Answer: _____

Probability

Aim: To solve problems involving probability

What You Need to Know

"Spinners" are often used in games of chance. Suppose you want to know your chance, or likelihood, for spinning a certain number. You would find your chance by finding the **probability** of spinning that number.

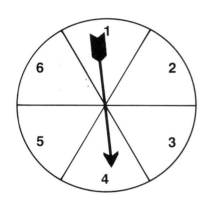

Probability is a number from 0 to 1. It tells how likely it is that an event will happen. Look at the spinner on this page.

- There are six *possible outcomes* on the spinner.
- Each region is the same size. So, the spinner is *equally likely* to stop in any one region.
- If you want to spin a 4, then spinning a 4 is called the *favorable outcome.*

To find the probability of something happening, use this formula:

$$\text{probability} = \frac{\text{number of favorable outcomes}}{\text{number of possible outcomes}}$$

Only one region on the spinner has a 4. So, there is only 1 favorable outcome. There are six regions on the spinner. So, there are 6 possible outcomes. The probability of spinning a 4 is $\frac{1}{6}$.

Think About It

What is the probability of spinning a 6?

_____

Read each problem. Use the spinner on this page for both Examples. Notice how the favorable outcomes and the possible outcomes are found.

Example A Find the probability of spinning a number greater than 4.
Number of Favorable Outcomes: *2*
Number of Possible Outcomes: *6*
Probability: $\frac{2}{6}$, *or* $\frac{1}{3}$

Example B Find the probability of spinning a number less than 5.
Number of Favorable Outcomes: *4*
Number of Possible Outcomes: *6*
Probability: $\frac{4}{6}$, *or* $\frac{2}{3}$

In Example A, there are two regions on the spinner carrying numbers greater than 4. These are the regions for 5 and 6. So, there are 2 favorable outcomes. There are six regions in all, so there are 6 possible outcomes.

In Example B, there are 4 favorable outcomes. The regions for 1, 2, 3, and 4 are all less than 5. Again, there are 6 possible outcomes.

Practice

Remember to follow all five problem solving steps as you solve these probability problems.

O	U	T	C	O	M	E	S

The letter-cards shown here are placed in a bag. Each card is made of the same material. Each card is shaped exactly the same. One card is picked without looking. Answer questions 1–4 about the drawings of letter-cards.

1. What is the probability of picking a T? _____

2. What is the probability of picking an O? _____

3. What is the probability of picking an O, U, or C? _____

4. What is the probability of picking an A? _____

5. There are 6 red marbles, 3 green marbles, and 1 blue marble in a jar. They are all the same except in color. You reach in the jar without looking and pick one marble. What is the probability of picking a green marble?

   _____

6. You toss a coin. What is the probability it lands on "heads"?

   _____

7. The numbers 1 through 6 are on a number cube. The cube is rolled. What is the probability of rolling an even number?

   _____

Lesson 30

Sales Tax

Aim: To solve problems by finding the sales tax on items and then computing the total cost

What You Need to Know

Cities and states need money to provide services. Their services include schools, police and fire departments, parks, libraries, and activity centers. One way to raise this money is to collect a tax. A **sales tax** is an amount of money added to the price of something you buy.

Use these formulas to find the amount of sales tax and then the total cost of an item. The rate of a sales tax is usually given as a percent.

sales tax = rate of sales tax × price of item
total cost = price + sales tax

Think About It

How is a sales tax rate usually shown? _____

Read each Example. Remember, when using a percent in a mathematical operation, change it to a decimal.

Example A Saul is buying a basketball for $12.50 plus 5% tax. What is the total cost of the basketball?

Sales Tax: *12.50*   **Total Cost:** *12.50*
                × .05   *+ .63*
          .6250, rounded up to .63   *13.13*

Answer: *$13.13*

Example B Peggy has $20. She wants to buy a baseball bat that costs $12.95 and a baseball that costs $5.95. There is a 6% sales tax. Can she buy the bat and ball?

Price of Items: *12.95*   **Sales Tax:** *18.90*
                   + 5.95   *× .06*
                    18.90   *1.1340*
                                          rounded down 1.13

Total Cost: *18.90*
               + 1.13
                20.03

Answer: *No, she cannot.*

In Example A, the sales tax rate (5%) is changed to a decimal (.05) before computing the amount of the sales tax. Notice that $.625 is rounded up to the nearest whole cent, $.63. The total cost is found by adding the price ($12.50) and the sales tax ($.63).

In Example B, the price of the bat and ball is found *before* computing the sales tax. The total cost is $20.03. Since Peggy has only $20, she cannot buy the bat and ball.

Practice

Solve each problem. Read the question carefully! Sometimes, you will need to find the amount of sales tax. Other times, you will need to find the total cost.

1. The price of a pair of jogging shoes is $32.95. The sales tax is 6%. Find the amount of tax.

   _____

2. Maria bought a warm-up jacket for $29.95 plus 4% sales tax. What was her total cost?

   _____

3. Tracy has $8. Can she buy swimming goggles that cost $7.50 plus 5% sales tax?

   _____

4. Frank wants to buy a tennis racket for $19.95 and a can of tennis balls for $2.99. There is a 5% sales tax. What will be the total cost of the racket and can of balls?

   _____

5. Steven bought a football for $21.50. Phil bought a soccer ball for $16.95. There is a 6% sales tax. How much more did Steven spend than Phil?

   _____

Additional word problems for Lesson 30 skills practice are on page 112.

73

Discounts

Aim: To solve problems by calculating the discount to find the sale price of items

What You Need to Know

At times a store will offer a **discount**. A discount is an amount of money that is subtracted from the original selling price. When you buy something on a discount, you pay less than usual. As with a sales tax, the rate of a discount is usually given as a percent. Use these formulas to find the amount of discount and the sale price.

discount = rate of discount × original price

sale price = original price − discount

Think About It

How do you find the discount on an item? _____

_____

Read each problem. Notice how the discount rate is changed from a percent to a decimal before multiplying.

one-day SALE

the Sound Shop

Example A The Sound Shop is having a one-day sale on all CDs. During the sale, Kate bought a classic rock CD that had an original price of $12.95. What was the sale price of the CD?

Discount: *12.95*
              × .15
       1.9425, rounded down $1.94

Sale Price: *12.95*
              −1.94
              11.01

Answer: *$11.01*

Classic Rock CDs **15% off**	Top 40 CDs **25% off**
Jazz and Blues CDs **20% off**	Blank tapes **30% off**

Example B Tina bought a CD of Broadway songs that was $3.00 off the original price of $15.00. What was the percent of the discount?

$$3.00 = n \times 15$$
$$\frac{3.00}{15} = n = .2$$

Answer: *20%*

In Example A, 15% is changed to .15 for use in the formula for finding the discount. Then the discount is subtracted from the original price to find the sale price.

In Example B, the formula for finding the discount is used again. This time, however, the formula is used to find the rate of discount, or the percent. Substitute the known values in the equation. Solve for the unknown value, *n*.

Practice

Solve each problem. Read the questions carefully!

1. Tim bought a jazz CD that originally sold for $14.50. What was the discount?

    _____

2. Anita bought a blank tape during the sale. The original price was $6.50. What was the sale price?

    _____

3. Jim bought two CDs. He bought a Top 40 CD that originally cost $18.00 and a blues CD that originally cost $12.00. What was the price of the two CDs together?

    _____

4. Earphones are on sale for $5 off the original price of $20. What is the percent of discount? (Hint: Look at Example B.)

    _____

5. A portable radio is on sale for $60. The original price was $75. What is the percent of discount? (Hint: First find the amount of discount.)

    _____

Time Cards

Aim: To solve problems involving time cards and hourly wages to find the money earned

What You Need to Know

A **time card** is a table set up to record the number of hours worked. Some workers get an **overtime rate** if they work more than the normal number of hours. Often, overtime is paid at "time and a half." This means the worker earns 1.5 times the normal hourly rate for each hour of overtime he or she works. The total amount earned is the sum of the overtime pay and the regular pay.

MAIN ST. SALON—Time Card

Name _Clay Osborne_

Week Ending _April 30_

	In	Out		In	Out	Hours Worked
Sun.						
Mon.	8:00	11:30	LUNCH	12:00	4:00	$7\frac{1}{2}$
Tues.	10:00	12:00		12:30	7:00	$8\frac{1}{2}$
Sat.	9:00	12:30		1:00	6:00	$8\frac{1}{2}$
					Total Hours	45

Think About It

How many hours did Clay work Tuesday? How many hours all week?

Read each problem. Notice how Clay's pay is calculated.

Example A Clay earns $5.50/hour. He gets time and a half for overtime. How much is he paid per hour of overtime?

The Plan: *1.5 × regular hourly pay = overtime pay*

The Execution:

$$\begin{array}{r} 5.50 \\ \times\ 1.5 \\ \hline 2750 \\ 550\ \\ \hline 8.250 \end{array}$$

Answer: *$8.25*

Example B Clay is paid overtime for work over 40 hours in a week. How much did he earn the week ending April 30?

The Plan: *regular pay + overtime pay = total pay*

The Execution:

$$\begin{array}{ccc} 5.50 & 8.25 & 220.00 \\ \times\ 40 & \times\ 5 & +\ 41.25 \\ \hline 220.00 & 41.25 & 261.25 \end{array}$$

Answer: *$261.25*

In Example A, multiply Clay's regular hourly pay by 1.5 to find his overtime hourly pay. In Example B, first find the amount Clay earned for the 40 hours worked at regular hourly pay. Then find the amount earned for the 5 hours of overtime. Clay's total weekly pay is the sum of his regular and his overtime pay.

Practice

Answer the questions about each time card.

1. Rosa earns $6.25 per hour at Best-Buy Food Mart. She is paid time and a half for overtime. How much does she earn for each hour of overtime?

   _____

2. Rosa is paid overtime for the time over 35 hours that she works. How much did Rosa earn during the week ending May 30?

   _____

BEST-BUY FOOD MART—Time Card

Name _Rosa Duke_

Week Ending _May 30_

	In	Out		In	Out	Hours Worked
Sun.						
Mon.	8:00	12:00	LUNCH	1:00	4:00	7
Tues.	9:00	1:00		1:30	4:30	7
Wed.	8:30	12:30		1:30	5:30	8
Thurs.	9:00	1:00		2:00	5:00	7
Fri.	10:00	2:00		3:00	7:00	8
Sat.	10:30	1:00				2.5
					Total Hours	39.5

3. Complete the "Hours Worked" column on the card for Mel Thomas.

4. Mel earns $10.50 per hour. He is paid time and a half for overtime. How much does he earn for each hour of overtime?

   _____

5. Mel is paid overtime for the time over 40 hours that he works. How much did Mel earn during the week ending June 30?

   _____

AUTO WORKS—Time Card

Name _Mel Thomas_

Week Ending _June 30_

	In	Out		In	Out	Hours Worked
Sun.						
Mon.	7:00	11:30	LUNCH	12:30	4:30	
Tues.	8:00	12:00		1:00	6:00	
Wed.	7:00	11:00		12:00	4:30	
Thurs.	7:00	11:30		12:30	4:00	
Fri.	7:00	12:00		1:00	3:00	
Sat.	8:00	12:00				
					Total Hours	

Additional word problems for Lesson 32 skills practice are on page 114.

Sampling

Aim: To solve problems by making predictions based on samples

What You Need to Know

 Sometimes you can use a **sample** of a group to answer questions about the whole group. This is done when it would be too hard (or not possible) to survey the whole group.

- To predict who will win an election, a newspaper may sample a group of voters.
- To decide what songs to play, a radio station may sample a group of listeners.

When a sample is used to make a prediction about a larger group, the sample must be *unbiased.* That is, it must truly reflect the whole group. Members of the sample must be picked at *random.*

Think About It

Suppose you wanted to learn the favorite sport of the students in your school. Which of these methods of picking people to ask would be biased: every third person in the hall or every fifth person in the stands at a basketball game?

Read each problem. Notice how the percent is found and then used to make a prediction.

Example A The school newspaper asked 50 randomly selected students to name their favorite kind of music. The results are shown in the chart. What percent of the students chose country music?

The Plan and Execution:

$$\frac{students\ choosing\ country\ music}{students\ in\ sample} \times 100 = percent$$

$$\frac{5}{50} = \frac{1}{10} = .10 \qquad .10 \times 100 = 10$$

Answer: *10%*

Example B There are 890 students in the school. Based on the sample, how many students in the school like country music best?

The Plan and Execution: *10% of 890 (.10 × 890 = 89)*

Answer: *89 students*

Favorite Music		
popular	~~HH~~ ~~HH~~ ~~HH~~ ~~HH~~ ~~HH~~	25
country	~~HH~~	5
jazz	~~HH~~ ~~HH~~	10
classical	//	2
other	~~HH~~ ///	8

In Example A, you find what percent of a sample answered a certain way. Once you know how a sample breaks down into percents, you can apply this breakdown to the whole group. (The whole group here is all the students in the school.) So, in Example B, you can say how many members of the whole group would answer in each category.

Practice

1. What percent of students in the sample on page 78 like popular music best?

   _____

2. There are 890 students in the school. Based on the sample, how many students in the school like popular music best?

   _____

3. In a random sample of 30 students, 6 walk to school. Based on this sample, how many of the 890 students can you predict walk to school?

   _____

CITY GAZETTE

Poll Results

Gomez	35
Hillard	55
Undecided	10

---

4. The local newspaper asked 100 voters for whom they planned to vote for city mayor. The results are shown in the chart. Based on the poll results, how many votes would you expect Hillard to receive if 15,000 people vote in the election?

   _____

5. In a random sample of 50 students, 6 said they were going to try out for the school band. There are 725 students in the school. Based on the sample, how many students can you predict will try out for the school band?

   _____

Unit 4 Review

A. On each line, write **T** or **F** to tell whether the statement is true or false.

_____ 1. Each time you write a check, you should add that amount of money to the balance in your checking account.

_____ 2. To find the "best buy" when shopping, you need to compare unit prices.

_____ 3. When you write a ratio to change a recipe, you compare the servings you need to the servings in the recipe.

_____ 4. A circle graph can help you to "see" a budget.

_____ 5. The sum of all the percents in a circle graph should be 50%.

_____ 6. Probability is a number between 0 and 100.

_____ 7. A sales tax is an amount of money subtracted from the price of something you buy.

_____ 8. To find the discount on an item, multiply the original price by the rate of the discount.

_____ 9. An overtime rate is paid to workers who have worked for a company for more than 1 year.

_____ 10. Sometimes you can use a sample of a group to answer questions about the whole group.

B. On each line, write the word that best completes the sentence.

_____ 11. A record of the checks you write and the deposits you make in your checking account is kept in a check ____.

_____ 12. The cost of one item, or the cost of one unit of an item, is called the ____ ____.

_____ 13. A plan for using money is called a ____.

_____ 14. A number that tells how likely it is that an event will happen is called a ____.

_____ 15. A time card is a table set up to record the number of ____ worked.

C. Circle the letter of the correct answer.

16. Doug had $250 in his checking account. He wrote a check for $23. How much money does he have in his checking account now?

    a. $273   **b.** $227   **c.** $233   **d.** $250

17. Katy had $415.25 in her checking account. She made a deposit of $35.13 into her checking account. How much money does she have in her checking account now?

    a. $440.38   **b.** $380.12   **c.** $450.38   **d.** $420.12

18. Find the unit price of potatoes if a 5-lb. bag of potatoes costs $1.20.

    a. $0.24 per pound   **b.** $0.24 per potato   **c.** $0.24 per bag   **d.** $0.24 per ounce

---
Waldorf Salad

1 cup diced celery
2 apples, diced
$\frac{1}{2}$ cup walnut pieces
$\frac{1}{2}$ cup mayonnaise
juice of 1 lemon

Mix ingredients.   Serves 4.

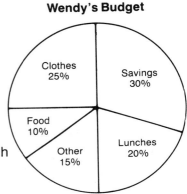

Wendy's Budget

19. How many apples are needed to make Waldorf salad for 12?

    a. 4 apples   **b.** 12 apples   **c.** 8 apples   **d.** 6 apples

20. Last week, Wendy earned $120. If she followed her budget, how much money did Wendy put away for savings?

    a. $36   **b.** $120   **c.** $30   **d.** $12

21. The numbers 1 through 6 are on a number cube. The cube is rolled. What is the probability of a 3 landing face up?

    a. $\frac{3}{6}$ **b.** $\frac{6}{6}$ **c.** $\frac{1}{6}$ **d.** $\frac{0}{6}$

22. Carla is buying a tennis racket for $35.95 plus 5% sales tax. What is the total cost of the tennis racket?

    a. $1.80   **b.** $34.15   **c.** $37.75   **d.** $36.75

23. Luis bought a book on sale for 25% off the original price. The original price was $7.80. What was the sale price?

    a. $1.95   **b.** $5.85   **c.** $9.75   **d.** $6.15

24. Liz earns $6.50/hour. She gets time and a half for time over 40 hours that she works. One week, Liz worked 43 hours. How much did she earn that week?

    a. $279.50   **b.** $419.25   **c.** $260.00   **d.** $289.25

25. In a random sample of 50 students, 30 students had pet dogs. There are 750 students in the school. Based on the sample, how many students in the school have pet dogs?

    a. 450 students   **b.** 550 students   **c.** 225 students   **d.** 425 students

---

Unit 4 Review (Continued)

D. Read and reread each word problem. Then follow the directions to show your solution to the problem.

Buy-Rite Foods	Food Fair
Applesauce 28-ounce jar $1.12	Applesauce 16-ounce jar $0.80

26. Look at the ads for applesauce. Which store has the better buy on applesauce?
   a. Underline the question.
   b. Circle the needed facts in the problem.

   c. Describe your plan: _____

   _____

   d. If an estimate can be made, show it here: _____

   e. Carry out your plan. Answer: _____

   f. Check your answer. If you got an incorrect answer, tell how you know it is wrong. Then write the correct answer.

   _____

   _____

27. Henry is buying a jacket for $39. There is a 5% sales tax. What is the total cost of the jacket?
   a. Underline the question.
   b. Circle the needed facts in the problem.

   c. Describe your plan: _____

   _____

   d. If an estimate can be made, show it here: _____

   e. Carry out your plan. Answer: _____

   f. Check your answer. If you got an incorrect answer, tell how you know it is wrong. Then write the correct answer.

   _____

   _____

82

Step One: Read the Problem

(pages 2–3)

Reword the question in each of the following word problems.

1. There are 75 people waiting to ride the elevator to the top of the city's tallest building. Only 30 people may ride on each trip. How many trips must the elevator make?

   The Question: _____

   _____

2. Guided tours of the building are given. Mr. Randall bought two adult tickets. How much did he spend?

   The Question: _____

   _____

Guided-Tour Tickets	
adults	$2.50
children	
6–12	$1.25
under 6	free

3. Mr. Chin went on the tour with his 8-year-old daughter and his 4-year-old son. How much did Mr. Chin spend for tickets?

   The Question: _____

   _____

4. One tour began at 1:15 P.M. and ended at 1:55 P.M. How long did the tour last?

   The Question: _____

   _____

5. Guidebooks cost $1.25. Rosa bought 3 guidebooks. How much did she spend?

   The Question: _____

   _____

6. There are plans to build 15 new buildings on 5 city blocks. The same number of buildings will be built on each block. How many buildings will be built on each block?

   The Question: _____

   _____

7. Each story in a building is about 12 feet high. About how tall will the 78-story building be?

   The Question: _____

   _____

Step Two: Find the Facts

(pages 4–5)

For each word problem, underline the question. Then write the facts you need to solve the problem.

1. Hobby Outlet sells three balls of twine for $0.81 and three skeins of yarn for $1.77. How much does one ball of twine cost?

   The Facts: _____

   _____

2. Saturday, 193 people came into the store. Of those, 76 people made purchases. How many people came into the store and did not buy anything?

   The Facts: _____

   _____

3. Max lives $4\frac{1}{4}$ miles from the Hobby Outlet. Ahmed lives $2\frac{1}{2}$ miles from the Hobby Outlet. Max rode his bike to the Outlet and then back home. How far did Max ride in all?

   The Facts: _____

   _____

BEAD SALE

	Regular Price	Sale Price
Plastic		
large	.24	.12
medium	.18	.09
Wooden		
large	.15	.09
medium	.12	.07

4. Rhonda bought 12 large wooden beads during the bead sale. How much did the beads cost?

   The Facts: _____

   _____

5. Last week, Joe paid the regular price for 10 large plastic beads. This week, he bought 10 more for the sale price. How much more did he pay for the beads last week?

   The Facts: _____

   _____

6. The Hobby Outlet is open from 9 A.M. to 9 P.M. on Monday through Saturday and from noon to 5 P.M. on Sunday. For how many hours is the store open in 1 week?

   The Facts: _____

   _____

Step Three: Plan What to Do
(pages 6–7)

For each problem, underline the question. Circle the needed facts. Then write a plan for solving the problem. Estimate the answer, if possible.

1. Mr. Gomez teaches 2 woodworking classes. There are 43 students in the 2 classes. There are 24 students in one class. How many students are in the other class?

   The Plan: _____

   The Estimate: _____

2. Each of the 43 students did 4 projects during the school year. How many projects were done by all the students during the year?

   The Plan: _____

   The Estimate: _____

3. Nancy has a board that is $7\frac{1}{2}$ feet long. She wants to cut the board to make 3 shelves that are the same length. How long will each shelf be?

   The Plan: _____

   The Estimate: _____

4. Julie spent 14 hours working on one project. She worked for $9\frac{3}{4}$ hours during class time and the rest of the time after school. How much time did Julie spend on her project after school?

   The Plan: _____

   The Estimate: _____

5. New ceiling tiles are being installed in the woodworking classroom. The classroom is 32 feet wide by 48 feet long. How many square feet of tile are needed for the ceiling?

   The Plan: _____

   The Estimate: _____

6. Marie cut a $27\frac{3}{8}$-inch piece from a board that was 1 yard long. How long was the piece of board that was left?

   The Plan: _____

   The Estimate: _____

Step Four: Carry Out the Plan

(pages 8–9)

Solve each problem. Be sure to follow all the steps you have learned.

1. Tim sells shoes at the Shoe Shop. He sold 52 pairs of shoes on Monday and 39 pairs on Tuesday. How many pairs did he sell in all on those 2 days?

2. Tim will earn a special bonus if he sells 75 pairs of boots. He has already sold 57 pairs. How many more must he sell to earn the bonus?

3. On Monday, Tim sold 10 pairs of slippers. The slippers were $7.95 a pair. How much money did he take in on the sale of slippers?

4. Shoes were on sale for $7.50 off the regular price. Marie bought a pair of shoes on sale for $15.45. What was the regular price of the shoes?

5. Fanta spent $50.85 for 3 pairs of shoes. What was the average price of each pair she bought?

6. Tim keeps the shoe boxes on shelves that are 65 inches long. Suppose a shoe box is 6.5 inches wide. How many boxes will fit on each shelf?

Super Sneaker Sale		
	Regular Price	Sale Price
High Flyers	$48.95	$39.00
Jumpers	$35.00	$27.99
Tennis Pros	$38.00	$30.39
Sport Line	$30.00	$24.00

7. Matt bought a pair of High Flyers and a pair of Tennis Pros during the Super Sneaker Sale. How much did he pay for the 2 pairs of shoes?

8. Phil bought 1 pair of Sport Line sneakers last week at the regular price. He bought another pair this week on sale. How much more did he pay for the sneakers last week?

9. Missy bought 3 pairs of Jumpers at the sale price. How much did she spend?

10. Tim usually works $33\frac{1}{2}$ hours a week. To be a full-time employee, he must work 40 hours each week. How many more hours must he work each week to be a full-time employee?

Step Five: Check the Answer

(pages 10–11)

For each problem, use the two-part check to decide if the computed answer is a correct answer. If it is correct, write it again. If it is incorrect, cross through it and write the correct answer.

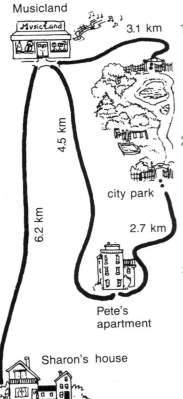

Musicland

3.1 km

4.5 km

6.2 km

city park

2.7 km

Pete's apartment

Sharon's house

1. Each Saturday, Sharon rides her bike from her house to Musicland for a piano lesson. After the lesson, she rides home the same way. How far does she ride in all to and from her lesson?

The Execution: 6.2
                  × 2
                 ─────
                 12.4

Computed Answer: 12.4 km

Correct Answer: _____

2. Pete rides a bus from his apartment to Musicland for guitar lessons. After each lesson, he rides the bus to City Park. Then he takes another bus from the park to his apartment. How far does Pete ride on the bus?

The Execution: 4.5
                  3.1
                + 2.7
                ─────
                10.2

Computed Answer: 10.2 km

Correct Answer: _____

3. How much farther does Sharon live from Musicland than Pete lives from Musicland?

The Execution: 6.2
                − 4.5
                ─────
                10.7

Computed Answer: 10.7 km

Correct Answer: _____

4. Pete practiced the guitar for $3\frac{1}{2}$ hours last week. What was the average amount of time he practiced each day?

The Execution: $3\frac{1}{2} \div 7 = \frac{7}{2} \times \frac{1}{7} = \frac{1}{2}$

Computed Answer: $\frac{1}{2}$ hour

Correct Answer: _____

5. Sharon is playing 3 songs in a recital. The first song takes $2\frac{1}{2}$ minutes. The second song takes $1\frac{3}{4}$ minutes. The third song takes 3 minutes. How long will Sharon be playing the piano in the recital?

The Execution: $2\frac{1}{2} + 1\frac{3}{4} + 3 = 6\frac{4}{6} = 6\frac{2}{3}$

Computed Answer: $6\frac{2}{3}$ min.

Correct Answer: _____

6. Sharon has been taking piano lessons for $2\frac{1}{2}$ years. Pete has taken guitar lessons 3 times longer than Sharon has taken piano lessons. For how long has Pete been taking guitar lessons?

The Execution: $2\frac{1}{2} \times 3 = \frac{5}{2} \times \frac{3}{1} = \frac{15}{2} = 7\frac{1}{2}$

Computed Answer: $7\frac{1}{2}$ years

Correct Answer: _____

Cumulative Practice: Steps 1, 2, 3, 4, and 5

(pages 12–13)

Follow all five steps to solve each problem. Don't forget to check your answers. Make sure they are all reasonable *and* accurate.

1. There were 2,643 adults and 1,296 children who attended a baseball game. How many people attended the game?

   _____

2. In the first game of the season, the home team had 13 hits and scored 7 runs. The visiting team had 15 hits and scored 5 runs. How many runs were scored in the first game?

   _____

3. Anita bowled 3 games. Her total score for the 3 games was 264 points. What was her average score for each game?

   _____

4. Teena jogged once around the track in 6 minutes, 11.5 seconds. Suppose she continued to jog at this same pace. How long would it take her to go around the track 4 times?

   _____

5. Carmen swam the 100-meter freestyle in 72.8 seconds. Margo swam the same distance in 77.2 seconds. How much faster was Carmen's time than Margo's time?

   _____

6. Paula spent $19.50 for 6 tickets to the hockey game. How much did each ticket cost?

   _____

7. During a 400-meter relay, Gary ran the first leg in 16.25 seconds. Barry ran the second leg in 18.43 seconds. Terry ran the third leg in 19.21 seconds. Jerry ran the fourth leg in 15.34 seconds. How long did it take the relay team to run the whole race?

   _____

8. On the first play of the football game, Les rushed for $13\frac{1}{2}$ yards. On the second play, Mark caught a pass for a $24\frac{1}{2}$-yard gain. How many yards were gained in these two plays?

   _____

9. During the game, the home team gained 98 yards rushing and 226 yards passing. How many more yards did they gain passing than rushing?

   _____

10. There are 33,800 seats in the ballpark. Suppose half of the seats are sold before game time. How many seats are left to be sold?

   _____

Too Much or Too Little Information
(pages 18–19)

If all the needed facts are given, solve the problem. If there is a missing fact, describe the fact you need.

1. Ann is in training for the swim team. Each day she does sit-ups and jogs $2\frac{3}{4}$ miles. How many sit-ups does she do in a week?

   _____

2. Pete does 15 sit-ups and 25 push-ups each day. Amir does twice as many sit-ups as Pete does. How many sit-ups does Amir do each day?

   _____

3. Flora bought a sweater for $12.95 and a shirt that was on sale for $7.25 off the regular price. How much did she pay for the shirt?

   _____

4. Jeff bought 3 belts that cost $5.49 each and 2 pairs of shoes that cost $19.95 each. How much did he spend on shoes?

   _____

5. Brad is 9 months old and weighs 18 pounds, 8 ounces. How much has he gained since birth?

   _____

6. It took Kate 5 days to paint her house. The paint she used cost $24.95 a gallon. How much did Kate spend on paint for her house?

   _____

7. There are 14,500 books in the local library. Most books may be checked out for 2 weeks. Reference books must be used in the library. How many books in the library may be checked out?

   _____

8. On Monday, Jenny spent $1\frac{1}{4}$ hours doing math homework and $\frac{3}{4}$ of an hour doing science homework. On Tuesday, she spent $\frac{1}{2}$ an hour doing math homework and $1\frac{3}{4}$ hours writing a book report. How much longer did she spend on math homework on Monday than on Tuesday?

   _____

9. Tom's computer printer cost $875. It can print 10 lines in 15 seconds. Phil's printer cost $450. It can print the same number of lines in half the time. How long does it take Phil's printer to print 10 lines?

   _____

Reading a Map

(pages 20–21)

Solve each problem. Use the map on page 20 for Problems 1–3.

_____

1. Jean drove from Sacramento through Yosemite Village to Fresno. How many miles did she drive?

_____

2. Assume a person wants to drive the shortest distance possible. How much farther is it from San Francisco to Crescent City than it is from San Francisco to Fresno?

_____

3. Carl made 3 round trips from San Bernardino to Bishop. How many miles did he drive on these trips?

Use the map on page 21 for Problems 4–6.

_____

4. Paul drove from Nashville through Knoxville and Asheville to Greensboro. How many miles did he drive in all?

_____

5. How much farther is it from Charlotte to Asheville than from Knoxville to Chattanooga?

_____

6. Three times a month, Chris drives from her home in Nashville to Chattanooga to Knoxville and back to Nashville. How many miles does she travel on these 3 trips?

_____

7. How much farther is it from Miami to Key West than it is from Miami to Naples?

_____

8. Dee drove from St. Petersburg to Tallahassee in 6 hours. She traveled the same number of miles each hour. How far did she drive each hour?

_____

9. Ken drives from Jacksonville to work in St. Augustine and back home again 5 days a week. How many miles does he drive to and from work each week?

Reading a Table

(pages 22–23)

Solve each problem. Use the table on page 22 for Problems 1–3.

_____ 1. Ruth rides the 6:15 A.M. train from Appleville to Oaksbury to work every day. How long is her ride to Oaksbury?

_____ 2. Phil rides the 8:30 A.M. train from Cedarton to Oaksbury. Then he has a 15-minute walk to work. What time does Phil get to work?

_____ 3. Al rides the 6:45 P.M. train from work in Oaksbury to his home in Cedarton each day. How long is his train ride home?

Use the table on page 23 for Problems 4–6.

_____ 4. Parma caught the 1:05 P.M. bus at Englewood and rode to Osprey. How long was her bus ride?

_____ 5. The 12:45 P.M. bus from North Port arrived at Sarasota Square Mall 3 minutes early. What time did the bus arrive at Sarasota Square Mall?

_____ 6. Betty caught the bus at Venice Hospital at 4:00 P.M. She got off the bus 25 minutes later. Where did Betty get off the bus?

Airline Schedules

From: Atlanta, GA	To: New York, NY		From: New York, NY	To: Denver, CO	
Departs	Arrives	Flight Number	Departs	Arrives	Flight Number
6:55 A.M.	9:00 A.M.	673	9:20 A.M.	11:50 A.M.	281
11:35 A.M.	1:40 P.M.	492	1:10 P.M.	3:20 P.M.	283
4:10 P.M.	6:20 P.M.	986	5:05 P.M.	7:15 P.M.	285
8:45 P.M.	10:50 P.M.	908			

_____ 7. Mary took the 4:10 P.M. flight from Atlanta to New York. How long was her flight?

_____ 8. The 8:45 P.M. flight from Atlanta to New York arrived 23 minutes late. What time did the flight arrive?

_____ 9. Flight number 283 from New York to Denver arrived 12 minutes early. What time did the flight arrive?

_____ 10. How much longer is the 9:20 A.M. flight from New York to Denver than the 5:05 P.M. flight from New York to Denver?

Reading a Graph

(pages 24–25)

Solve each problem. Use the graph on page 24 for Problems 1–3.

_____

1. In Boston, how many degrees warmer is the monthly normal temperature in August than in September?

_____

2. One day in January, the temperature was 18 degrees below the normal for January. How low did the temperature go on that day?

_____

3. One day in July, the high temperature was 91 °F. How many degrees above the monthly normal for July was the temperature that day?

Use the graph on page 25 for Problems 4–6.

_____

4. How many degrees warmer was the high temperature on Sunday than the low temperature on Sunday?

_____

5. Forecasters are predicting that the low temperature on Saturday will be 5 degrees higher than the low temperature for Friday. What is the low temperature on Saturday predicted to be?

_____

6. How many degrees cooler was the low temperature on Tuesday than the low temperature on Sunday?

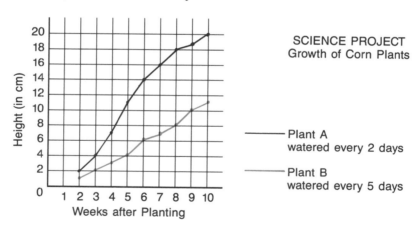

SCIENCE PROJECT
Growth of Corn Plants

_____ Plant A
watered every 2 days

_____ Plant B
watered every 5 days

_____

7. How many centimeters did Plant A grow between the second and fourth weeks?

_____

8. Suppose Plant A grows 3 centimeters between the tenth and eleventh weeks. How tall will it be after the eleventh week?

_____

9. How many centimeters taller was Plant A than Plant B after 10 weeks?

_____

10. How many centimeters shorter was Plant B than Plant A after 4 weeks?

Using the Appendix

(pages 26–27)

Solve each problem. Refer to the Appendix if you need to.

_____ 1. Today is Chen's birthday. He is 13 years old. How many weeks old is Chen?

_____ 2. A circular table top has a radius of 2 feet. What is the area of the table top? (Use 3.14 for π.)

_____ 3. The base of a triangular piece of tile is 56 millimeters. Its height is 64 millimeters. What is the area of the tile?

_____ 4. A quarter weighs about 5 grams. About how many quarters are in a bag that weighs 2 kilograms?

_____ 5. A mall was built on $1\frac{1}{2}$ square miles of land. How many acres of land were used for the mall?

_____ 6. A box is 2.5 meters long, 1.5 meters wide, and 1 meter high. What is the volume of the box?

_____ 7. An empty airplane weighs about 150 tons. Suppose 60 tons of fuel and cargo are put on the plane. About how many pounds does the loaded plane weigh?

_____ 8. Jill is making orange juice. She has 8 cans of frozen juice. Each can is mixed with water to make $1\frac{1}{2}$ quarts of juice. How many gallons of juice will the 8 cans make?

_____ 9. Sherrie wants to build a rectangular pen for her rabbit. The pen will be 9 feet long and 4 feet wide. How many feet of fencing does she need?

_____ 10. What will be the area of the rabbit pen in Problem 9 in square yards?

Choosing the Operation

(pages 28–29)

Solve each problem.

_____ 1. When you exercise, your heart pumps about 1.8 gallons of blood each minute. About how many gallons does your heart pump during 1 hour of exercise?

_____ 2. When you rest, your heart pumps about 48 gallons of blood in 1 hour. About how many gallons does your heart pump during each minute of rest?

_____ 3. After Rose jogged, her heart beat 150 times per minute. How many times per second did her heart beat?

_____ 4. After Rose rested, her heart beat 1.5 times per second. How many times per minute did her heart beat?

_____ 5. Luis breathes at a rate of 19 breaths per minute. How many breaths does Luis breathe in 1 hour?

_____ 6. In a healthy adult, the right lung weighs about 620 grams. The left lung weighs about 570 grams. How much more does the right lung weigh than the left lung?

_____ 7. The daily amount of calcium in a diet should be 1.4 grams. One cup of whole milk contains 0.28 gram of calcium. How many cups of whole milk per day will supply the daily amount?

_____ 8. One cup of milk contains 0.28 gram of calcium. Two slices of bread contain 0.04 gram of calcium. One slice of chicken contains 0.01 gram of calcium. Suppose you have a chicken sandwich and a cup of milk for lunch. How many grams of calcium will you eat?

_____ 9. One cup of carrots contains about 0.9 milligram of iron. One cup of spinach contains about 4 milligrams of iron. How much more iron is in a cup of spinach than is in a cup of carrots?

_____ 10. One egg contains 1.4 milligrams of iron. A banana contains 0.6 milligram of iron. A bowl of cereal contains 0.8 milligram of iron. Mel ate an egg and a banana. How many milligrams of iron did she eat?

Two-Operation Problems

(pages 30–31)

Solve each problem. Use the calorie chart on page 30 if you need to.

1. To make a sandwich, Don used 2 slices of white bread and 2 slices of Swiss cheese. How many calories were in the sandwich?

2. How many more calories are in $\frac{1}{2}$ grapefruit than in $\frac{1}{2}$ cantaloupe?

3. Beth used 1 banana, 1 apple, 1 peach, 1 cup of strawberries, and 1 cup of yogurt to make a fruit salad for 5 people. How many calories were in each serving?

4. A loaf of bread contains 20 slices. How many more calories are there in a loaf of white bread than a loaf of whole wheat bread?

5. Bud wants to eat no more than 2,800 calories per day. One day he ate a 565-calorie breakfast and a 725-calorie lunch. How many more calories could he eat that day and still stay within his goal?

6. To lose 1 pound of fat, a person must cut back about 3,000 calories. Suppose you want to lose 3 pounds in 12 days. How many calories will you have to cut back each day?

7. On Monday, Jim ate 2,200 calories. On Tuesday, he ate 2,750 calories. On Wednesday, he ate 2,550 calories. What was the average number of calories he ate per day during those 3 days?

8. Marge had a blueberry muffin and an orange for breakfast. She had an apple and a cup of skim milk for a snack. How many more calories did she eat for breakfast than for the snack?

9. One gram of fat contains 9 calories. One gram of carbohydrate or protein contains 4 calories. How many total calories are in 12 grams of fat, 12 grams of carbohydrates, and 12 grams of protein?

10. How many more calories are in 10 grams of fat than in 10 grams of protein? (Use the facts you need in Problem 9.)

Multiple-Step Problems

(pages 32–33)

Solve each problem.

_____

1. Carlo bought 2 adult tickets and 3 children's tickets for the afternoon show. He gave the cashier at the ticket window $20. How much change did he get?

_____

2. How much more does it cost to buy 2 adult tickets and 2 children's tickets to the evening show than to the afternoon show?

```
          TRI-CINEMA
    afternoon shows  2 PM
      adults        $5.50
      children      $3.00
    evening shows
      adults        $7.50
      children      $6.00
```

_____

3. For one afternoon show, Tri-Cinema sold 237 adult tickets and 356 children's tickets. How much less than $3,000 did the theater collect?

_____

4. For one evening show, Tri-Cinema sold 315 adult tickets and 129 children's tickets. How much more than $3,000 did the theater collect?

_____

5. There are 3 movie theaters at Tri-Cinema. Theater I seats 50 fewer people than Theater II. Theater II seats twice as many people as Theater III. Theater III seats 360 people. How many people does Theater I seat?

_____

6. For one show, Theater I sold 250 tickets. Theater II sold 310 tickets. Theater III sold 190 tickets. How many empty seats were left in all three theaters? (Use the facts you need in Problem 5.)

_____

7. The theater owner has set aside $5,000 to replace one-half of the 360 seats in Theater III. The new seats will cost $45 each. How much more money will the owner need to set aside?

_____

8. There are 5 shows in each of the 3 theaters on Saturday. There are 4 shows in each of the 3 theaters on Sunday through Friday. How many shows are there altogether in the 3 theaters during a week?

_____

9. At the snack bar, Matt bought 3 boxes of popcorn for $1.75 each. He also bought 3 cups of grape juice for $1.50 each. How much change did he get from $10.00?

_____

10. Donna bought 4 tickets to an afternoon show. She gave the cashier $15.00 and got $0.50 in change. How many adult and how many children's tickets did she buy?

Checking Estimates and Computations
(pages 34–35)

Solve each problem. Show an estimated answer and a computed answer for each.

1. Plants Galore is having a sale. Maxine bought a hanging basket for $7.95 and a clay pot for $3.75. How much did she spend in all?

    Estimated Answer: _____   Computed Answer: _____

2. Beth has a $24.00 gift certificate from Plants Galore. How many lily plants for $3.95 each can she buy with her gift certificate?

    Estimated Answer: _____   Computed Answer: _____

3. Joel works 38 hours a week at Plants Galore. He earns $4.95 per hour. How much does he earn in a week?

    Estimated Answer: _____   Computed Answer: _____

4. Plants Galore is open 50 hours a week. It is open 8 hours a day on Monday through Friday and 6 hours on Saturday. How many hours is it open on Sunday?

    Estimated Answer: _____   Computed Answer: _____

5. Pete buys 3 ferns for $3.95 each and 12 cactus for $1.09 each. How much does he spend in all?

    Estimated Answer: _____   Computed Answer: _____

6. Jake paid $8.29 for 6 ivy plants and a bag of soil. The soil cost $2.95. How much did each ivy plant cost?

    Estimated Answer: _____   Computed Answer: _____

7. Lara bought 3 plants for $1.79 each. How much change did she get from $10?

    Estimated Answer: _____   Computed Answer: _____

8. Rudy owes Plants Galore $49. He makes a $17 payment. He agrees to pay the rest in 4 weekly payments. How much will he pay each week?

    Estimated Answer: _____   Computed Answer: _____

9. The owners of Plants Galore bought 50 hanging baskets for $4.95 each. They sold the baskets for $7.25 each. How much profit did they make on the sale of the 50 baskets?

    Estimated Answer: _____   Computed Answer: _____

Making a Diagram

(pages 40–41)

Solve each problem. Draw diagrams to help you.

_____ 1. In a hamster cage, it is 65 cm from the exercise wheel to the food cup. A hamster gets off the wheel, walks 20 cm toward the food, turns around, and goes back to the wheel. Then it walks 30 cm toward the food, turns around, and goes back to the wheel. Finally, it walks straight from the wheel to the food cup. How far does the hamster walk in all?

_____ 2. Anne can play the piano and the flute. Barb can play the guitar and the drums. Carla can play the banjo and the violin. If each person plays one of her two instruments, how many combinations of three-instrument play are possible?

_____ 3. There are 5 candidates running for class president. Before the election, each candidate shakes hands with all the other candidates. How many handshakes are there?

_____ 4. For his science project, Marty is growing bean seeds in paper cups. He will test the following conditions—soil, food, and light. He will plant seeds in loam, sand, and clay. He will add plant food and he will not add plant food. He will place seeds in light and in shade. How many cups will he need to try all possible tests?

_____ 5. Nikki is putting a fence around her rectangular garden. The garden is $16\frac{1}{2}$ feet by $27\frac{1}{2}$ feet. Nikki is spacing fence posts $5\frac{1}{2}$ feet apart. How many posts will she need?

_____ 6. Phil lives 3.5 kilometers from Burger Cafe. Central Park is 2.8 kilometers from Burger Cafe. Phil roller-skated from his house to Burger Cafe for lunch. He then skated to Central Park. On his way home, he stopped at Burger Cafe for water. Then he skated home. How far did Phil skate in all?

_____ 7. Jean got into an elevator. She went down 6 floors, up 7 floors, and down 8 floors. She was then on the fifth floor. On what floor did Jean get on the elevator?

_____ 8. Tanya lives 3 blocks from Julie and $4\frac{1}{2}$ blocks from Debbie. Debbie's apartment is $1\frac{1}{2}$ blocks from Mort's Market. Tanya walked to Julie's house. Together the two girls walked back to Tanya's house. Then they walked to Debbie's apartment. The three girls then walked to Mort's Market. How far did Tanya walk in all?

_____ 9. A spider is climbing up a 12-foot pole. It climbs 3 feet at a time and then stops to rest. Each time it stops to rest, it slips back $\frac{1}{2}$ foot. The spider starts at the bottom of the pole. How many times will it stop to rest before it reaches the top of the pole?

_____ 10. Brad has 100 square tiles to make a square table top. Each tile is 1 inch on a side. Brad will leave $\frac{1}{8}$ inch between tiles when he makes the table top. How long will each side of the table top be?

Making a Line Graph
(pages 42–43)

Solve each problem. Make line graphs to help you.

_____ 1. Heather's car can go 55 miles on 2 gallons of gas. How many miles will the car travel on 6 gallons of gas?

_____ 2. How many gallons of gas does Heather's car need to travel 220 miles?

_____ 3. The cost to rent a bike at Rent-All is $7 for 2 days. How much will it cost to rent a bike for 8 days?

_____ 4. Bud has $42. For how many days may he rent a bike from Rent-All?

_____ 5. Paul is driving to Rock City. He leaves at 7 A.M. and drives at a speed of 60 kilometers per hour. Paul's mother leaves from the same house and follows the same route to Rock City. She leaves at 8 A.M. and drives at 80 kilometers per hour. Paul has driven 180 kilometers. What time is it?

_____ 6. How far will Paul's mother have driven by 10 A.M.?

_____ 7. At what time will Paul and his mother meet on the highway?

_____ 8. A mother cat and her fastest kitten are running along the same street. The kitten starts 15 meters in front of its mother. The kitten runs at 5 meters per second. The mother cat runs at 8 meters per second. How far will the mother cat have gone in 3 seconds?

_____ 9. How long will it take the mother cat to go 32 meters?

_____ 10. How many seconds will it take the mother cat to catch her kitten?

Writing an Equation

(pages 44–45)

For each problem, write an equation and solve.

1. Mr. Lopez ordered 150 pairs of jogging shoes for his sports store. He received 85 pairs of shoes. How many more pairs of shoes does he need to complete his order?

   Equation: _____   Answer: _____

2. Vera and Jason work part-time at the sports store. Last week, Vera worked 20 hours. This is $2\frac{1}{2}$ times the number of hours Jason worked. How many hours did Jason work?

   Equation: _____   Answer: _____

3. Marge spends $14.94 for 6 pairs of socks. How much does each pair of socks cost?

   Equation: _____   Answer: _____

4. Beth has saved $36.00 to buy a new tennis racket. This is $\frac{2}{3}$ of what she needs to buy the racket. How much does the new racket cost?

   Equation: _____   Answer: _____

5. Soccer balls are on sale for $13.45. This is $4.50 off the regular price. What is the regular price?

   Equation: _____   Answer: _____

6. Steve spent $69.44 for 2 pairs of knee pads and a skateboard. The knee pads cost $4.95 a pair. How much did the skateboard cost?

   Equation: _____   Answer: _____

7. Mr. Lopez ordered 4 times as many baseballs as bats for his store. He ordered 180 baseballs. How many bats did he order?

   Equation: _____   Answer: _____

8. Softballs cost $.75 more than baseballs. The softballs cost $4.95 each. How much do baseballs cost?

   Equation: _____   Answer: _____

9. Maria bought 3 cans of tennis balls and a visor for $13.89. The tennis balls cost $2.98 a can. How much did the visor cost?

   Equation: _____   Answer: _____

Using a Formula

(pages 46–47)

Use the formulas listed on page 46 or in the Appendix on page 121 to help you solve these problems.

_____ 1. A plane flew at an average speed of 580 mph from Los Angeles to New York in $4\frac{1}{4}$ hours. How far did the airplane fly?

_____ 2. A bus traveled 120 miles from New York to Hartford in $2\frac{1}{2}$ hours. What was the average rate of speed the bus traveled?

_____ 3. Robyn began jogging at 9 A.M. She jogged at a rate of 4 miles per hour for 6 miles. What time did she stop jogging?

_____ 4. Corey invested $2,500 at 6% simple interest for $4\frac{1}{2}$ years. How much interest did he earn?

_____ 5. Fran borrowed $750 at 11.5% simple interest. For how long did she borrow the money if the interest she paid was $172.50?

_____ 6. Chris invested $1,200 at simple interest. After 3 years, she had earned $270. What was the interest rate?

_____ 7. John borrowed some money from a bank for 5 years at a simple interest rate of 12.5%. He paid $3,125 in interest for the 5 years. How much money did John borrow?

_____ 8. A circular table top has a diameter of 4 feet. What is the area of the table top?

_____ 9. The area of a rectangular rug is 108 square feet. The rug is 9 feet wide. How long is the rug?

_____ 10. The volume of a shipping carton is 24 cubic feet. The carton is 2 feet wide and 3 feet long. How high is the carton?

Solving a Simpler Problem

(pages 48–49)

Solve each problem by thinking of a similar but simpler problem.

_____ 1. How many ways can you add 3 numbers to get a sum of 6? (Here are three ways: 6 + 0 + 0, 5 + 0 + 1, 5 + 1 + 0.)

_____ 2. How many ways can you add 3 numbers to get a sum of 12?

_____ 3. How many ways can you add 4 numbers to get a sum of 5?

_____ 4. How many triangles are in this figure?

_____ 5. Suppose 1 road is built to connect a single pair of cities. (Each road can connect only 2 cities.) What is the largest number of roads that could be built to connect 12 cities?

_____ 6. How many squares are in this figure?

_____ 7. Nikki and Lori live 152 kilometers apart. They plan to leave their homes at the same time and ride toward each other. Nikki will ride at 16 kilometers per hour. Lori will ride at 22 kilometers per hour. At what time must they leave their homes in order to meet for lunch exactly at noon?

_____ 8. How many triangles are in this figure?

_____ 9. Benny is starting a computer club. He is the only member now. He plans to have each member bring in 2 new members each month. Suppose his plan works. How many members will the club have at the end of 6 months?

_____ 10. How many angles are in this figure? (AOB, AOC, and BOL are 3 angles.)

Using Ratio Proportions
(pages 50–51)

Write a proportion for each problem. Then solve. Use the scale drawing on page 50 for Problems 1–3.

_____ 1. What are the actual dimensions (length and width) of the smaller bedroom in Beth's apartment?

_____ 2. What are the actual outside dimensions of Beth's apartment?

_____ 3. Beth is going to add a patio that is 4.5 meters wide. She will use the same scale used for the apartment. How wide will the patio be in her scale drawing?

_____ 4. A 747 jet airliner is about 225 feet long. It has a wingspan of about 200 feet. A scale model of the plane is 18 inches long. What is the wingspan of the model?

_____ 5. A scale model of a steam locomotive is 11 inches long. The ratio of the model to the actual train is 1 to 48. What is the length of the actual locomotive?

_____ 6. An airplane travels 1,800 miles in 4 hours. At this rate, how far will it go in 6 hours?

_____ 7. The ratio of students with blue eyes to students with brown eyes is 3 to 2. Twelve students have brown eyes. How many students have blue eyes?

_____ 8. Al can type 2 pages in 15 minutes. How many pages can he type in 2 hours?

_____ 9. Joan is a softball pitcher. She strikes out 3 of every 7 batters she faces. Suppose she faces 42 batters. How many strikeouts does she have?

_____ 10. Carlos read 25 pages in 45 minutes. How many hours will it take him to read 200 pages?

Using Logical Reasoning

(pages 52–53)

Use logical reasoning to solve each problem.

1. Rosa, Stan, and Tom each play a different instrument. They play a flute, a guitar, and a trumpet.
   Clue 1: Stan and the trumpet player walk to school together.
   Clue 2: Tom loves to sing while his friend plays the guitar.
   Clue 3: Rosa will play the flute in a concert next week.
   What instrument does Tom play?

2. Marcy, Thad, Carlotta, and Jake each enjoy playing a different sport. They play baseball, basketball, football, and volleyball. One of Marcy's friends in the group plays basketball. Carlotta and Jake do not play volleyball. Thad enjoys playing football. Jake used to like playing baseball but has changed his favorite. Who plays volleyball?

3. Tim, Jim, Kim, and Sim ran a race. At the end of the race, Tim was 20 yards behind Jim. Jim was 50 yards ahead of Kim. Sim was 30 yards ahead of Kim. Who won the race?

4. You have 20 coins to arrange in 4 stacks. All the stacks have an even number of coins. The second stack has twice as many coins as the fourth stack. Each stack has a different number of coins. Each stack has at least 1 coin. The third stack has the most coins. How many coins are in each stack?

   1st stack _____ ; 2nd stack _____ ; 3rd stack _____ ; 4th stack _____

5. A rowboat can carry only 175 pounds. Jean weighs 125 pounds. Joan weighs 100 pounds. Jan weighs 75 pounds. Jean, Joan, and Jan are together on one side of a lake. How may they use the rowboat to cross the lake?

   _____

   _____

6. Suppose you have a 3-quart pail and an 8-quart pail. There are no markings on either pail. How may you use these pails to get exactly 4 quarts of water in the larger pail?

   _____

   _____

   _____

   _____

Exact or Estimated Answers

(pages 54–55)

For each problem, first decide whether an exact or an estimated answer is necessary. Then solve the problem.

_____   1. Denise has a 312-page book to read in 6 days. Suppose she reads 45 pages each day. Will she finish the book in 6 days?

_____   2. The population of Phoenix, Arizona, increased from 106,818 in 1950 to 789,704 in 1980. About how many more people lived in Phoenix in 1980 than in 1950?

_____   3. Mavis bought 3 books that cost $4.98, $5.29, and $3.29. The clerk added $0.68 tax. Mavis paid for the books with a check. For how much was the check?

_____   4. Brad has a part-time job. He has saved $85 to buy a new stereo and head-phones. The stereo costs $59.95. The headphones cost $18.99. Has Brad saved enough money?

_____   5. Each shelf in the library has about 25 books. There are 1,197 shelves of books in the library. About how many books are in the library?

_____   6. Mark bought 3 pounds of tomatoes for $0.79 per pound and 1 head of let-tuce for $0.69. He gave the clerk the correct amount of money. How much did he give the clerk?

_____   7. Claire works at least 20 hours each week. Last week, she worked $4\frac{1}{2}$ hours each on Monday, Wednesday, and Friday. She worked $5\frac{1}{2}$ hours each on Tuesday and Thursday. Did Claire work more than or less than 20 hours last week?

_____   8. Jenny walks $8\frac{1}{4}$ blocks each way to and from school each day. About how many blocks does she walk during a 5-day school week?

_____   9. Pete needs 18 milligrams of iron in his diet each day. He had 4.6 milli-grams for breakfast and 6.3 milligrams for lunch. How many more milli-grams does he need?

_____ 10. Lou has $23\frac{1}{2}$ yards of fabric to make covers for furniture. He needs $16\frac{1}{4}$ yards for a sofa, $3\frac{1}{2}$ yards for a chair, and $1\frac{3}{4}$ yards for a stool. Does Lou have enough fabric?

More Than One Strategy

(pages 56–57)

Use whatever strategy works best for you to solve each problem.

_____ 1. Books are sale priced at 3 for $9.99. At that rate, how much will 5 books cost?

_____ 2. Nancy left Hometown at 9 A.M. She drove at an average speed of 25 miles per hour. Jill followed her 1 hour later, driving at an average speed of 35 miles per hour. About what time did Jill overtake Nancy?

_____ 3. A piece of land costs $30,000. That is $2\frac{1}{2}$ times as much as it cost in 1980. How much did the land cost in 1980?

_____ 4. Six students played in the chess tournament. Each student played every other student once. How many games were played?

_____ 5. A bus is traveling at an average speed of 45 miles per hour. How far will it travel in 3 hours?

_____ 6. Burger Cafe sells 6 kinds of burgers with a choice of 3 sauces and a choice of 2 kinds of rolls. How many choices are there for a burger with sauce on a roll?

_____ 7. Mel invested $750 at $6\frac{1}{2}$% simple interest for 2 years. How much interest did she earn?

_____ 8. A map is drawn with a scale of 2 inches = 30 miles. Suppose an actual road is 45 miles long. How long will the road be on the map?

9. Al, Barb, Cal, and Dee swam a relay. At the end of the race,
   Dee was 2 yards ahead of Al.
   Al was 1 yard behind Barb.
   Barb was 3 yards ahead of Cal.
   In what order did the four finish the race?

   1st place _____; 2nd place _____; 3rd place _____; 4th place _____

_____ 10. Rose spent $5\frac{1}{2}$ hours working on her science project. This is $2\frac{1}{4}$ hours more than Teena spent on her science project. How long did Teena spend on her project?

Checking Accounts

(pages 62–63)

Answer these questions about checks and check registers.

1. Sherry has $114.69 in her checking account. She writes a check to Green Thumb Nursery for $35.79. How much money does Sherry have left in her checking account?

2. Joel has $57.13 in his checking account. He deposited $125.75. How much money does he have in his checking account now?

This is Pam's check register.

NUMBER	DATE	DESCRIPTION OF TRANSACTION	PAYMENT/DEBIT (–)		DEPOSIT/CREDIT (+)		BALANCE	
							$ 328	69
204	4/12	The Food Mart	$ 13	50	$		315	19
	4/15	Deposit			125	50		
205	4/16	Beeline Buslines	63	95				
206	4/18	General Telephone	24	69				

3. What was Pam's balance after she made the deposit on April 15? Write the new balance on the register.

4. What was the balance after Pam wrote check number 205? Write the new balance on the register.

5. What was Pam's balance after her check to General Telephone? Write the new balance on the register.

6. On April 30, Pam wrote check number 207 to The Music Shop for $13.95. Complete the register for this check.

7. On May 2, Pam made a deposit of $25.13 into her checking account. Complete the register for this deposit.

8. Bob wrote a check for $20.89 on April 3, 1987. He made the check out to SportLine to pay for a new soccer ball and knee pads. Complete Bob's check.

```
                                                                    103
            Bob Duke
            789 Hills Street
            Our Town, U.S.A.              _____ 19_____

PAY TO THE
ORDER OF _____ $ [        ]

_____ DOLLARS

        Statewide Savings

MEMO _____          _____
```

Unit Pricing
(pages 64–65)

For Problems 1–5, find the unit price to the nearest cent.

1. 3 grapefruit for $0.89: _____

2. 3 pounds of potatoes for $1.29: _____

3. 4-pack of light bulbs for $2.19: _____

4. 16-ounce can of peanuts for $2.69: _____

5. 1 dozen eggs for $0.89: _____

For Problems 6–11, find the unit prices. Then tell which item is the better buy.

6. 3-lb. bag of apples for $1.89 *or* a 5-lb. bag of apples for $3.25

   Better Buy: _____

7. package of 8 corn muffins for $1.59 *or* package of 12 corn muffins for $1.99

   Better Buy: _____

8. 8-oz. bottle of salad dressing for $1.09 *or* 20-oz. bottle of salad dressing for $2.39

   Better Buy: _____

9. 9-oz. box of rice for $1.29 *or* 13-oz. box of rice for $2.08

   Better Buy: _____

10. 6 oranges for $0.79 *or* 8 oranges for $0.95

    Better Buy: _____

11. 11-oz. box of cereal for $1.69 *or* 15-oz. box of cereal for $2.12

    Better Buy: _____

For Problems 12–14, answer the question.

_____ 12. Three cans of LiteLine juice sell for $0.69. Eight cans of Zippy juice sell for $1.60. You buy 12 cans of the better buy. How much do you spend?

_____ 13. A 16-oz. loaf of All-Grain Bread sells for $0.64. A 20-oz. loaf of Natural Bread sells for $1.00. You buy 3 loaves of the better buy. How much do you spend?

_____ 14. One pound of DairyLine Swiss cheese costs $2.48. One and one-half pounds of Best Buy Swiss cheese cost $3.87. You buy 2.5 pounds of the better buy. How much do you spend?

Recipes
(pages 66–67)

Solve each problem. Use the recipe on page 66 for Problems 1–3.

_____ 1. How much ground beef is needed to make a meat loaf for 3 people?

_____ 2. How much milk is needed to make a meat loaf for 6 people?

_____ 3. How much pepper is needed to make a meat loaf for 12 people?

Use the recipe on page 67 for Problems 4–7.

_____ 4. How many eggs are needed to make 27 banana oatmeal muffins?

_____ 5. How much cooking oil is needed to make 9 muffins?

_____ 6. How much honey is needed to make 36 muffins?

_____ 7. What amount of oats is needed to make 12 muffins?

Use this recipe for Problems 8–12.

```
┌─────────────────────────────────────────────────────────┐
│                    Glazed Carrots                          │
│                                                            │
│  2 cups cooked, sliced carrots    1 tablespoon lemon juice │
│  4 tablespoons margarine          1 teaspoon chopped parsley│
│  1½ teaspoons brown sugar                                  │
│                                                            │
│  Melt margarine in pan. Add sugar and lemon juice. Mix well.│
│  Stir in carrots. Shake pan to glaze carrots. Place in serving│
│  bowl and garnish with parsley.              Serves 6      │
└─────────────────────────────────────────────────────────┘
```

_____ 8. What amount of carrots is needed to prepare glazed carrots for 9 people?

_____ 9. How much margarine is needed to prepare glazed carrots for 3 people?

_____ 10. How much brown sugar is needed to prepare glazed carrots for 12 people?

_____ 11. How much lemon juice is needed to prepare glazed carrots for 3 people?

_____ 12. How many people may be served from a recipe using 5 cups of sliced carrots?

Budgets

(pages 68–69)

Answer each question. Use the circle graph on page 68 for Problems 1–3.

_____

1. Suppose Gina earns $82. How much may she spend on recreation?

_____

2. Last week Gina worked 5 days and earned $88. It cost Gina $1.25 each way to ride the bus to and from her part-time job. Did Gina stay within her budget for transportation last week?

_____

3. One week Gina earned $78. The next week she earned $96. How much did she save for the two weeks?

Use the circle graph on page 69 for Problems 4–6. The Simons used the same plan to budget their money last year when their combined take-home pay was $32,500.

_____

4. How much money did the Simons budget for food last year?

_____

5. How much money did the Simons budget for clothing and transportation together last year?

_____

6. How much more money did the Simons budget for housing than for food?

Pablo has a part-time job at the Bike Shop. This circle graph shows how he budgets the money he earns.

Pablo's Budget

- Gifts 10%
- Other 5%
- Entertainment 20%
- Food 15%
- Savings 30%
- Clothing 20%

_____

7. One week Pablo earned $95. How much did he save?

_____

8. Suppose Pablo earns $88. How much more may he spend on clothing than on food?

_____

9. Last week Pablo earned $83. This week he earned $72. He wants to buy his brother a radio that costs $12.95. Suppose he used the money budgeted for gifts last week and this week. Can he buy the radio?

_____

10. This month Pablo has earned $338. He used money budgeted for clothing to buy a jacket for $29.95. He wants to buy a warm-up suit for $39.95. Can he buy the warm-up suit and stay within his budget for this month?

Probability

(pages 70–71)

Solve these probability problems. Use the spinner on page 70 for Problems 1–3.

_____ 1. What is the probability of spinning a 1 or a 2?

_____ 2. What is the probability of spinning an 8?

_____ 3. What is the probability of spinning a number less than 8?

| F | A | V | O | R | A | B | L | E |

These letter cards are placed in a bag. Each card is made of the same material. Each card is shaped exactly the same. One card is picked without looking. Answer Problems 4–7 about the letter cards.

_____ 4. What is the probability of picking a V?

_____ 5. What is the probability of picking an A?

_____ 6. What is the probability of picking a vowel?

_____ 7. What is the probability of picking a consonant?

There are 8 green blocks, 6 yellow blocks, 4 red blocks, and 2 white blocks in a bag. They are all the same except in color. Imagine picking a block without looking. Answer Problems 8–10 about the blocks.

_____ 8. What is the probability of picking a green block?

_____ 9. What is the probability of picking a yellow block or a red block?

_____ 10. What is the probability of picking a purple block?

_____ 11. There are 6 red socks and 2 blue socks in a drawer. Imagine picking 1 sock without looking. What is the probability that the sock will be blue?

_____ 12. These numbers are placed on the faces of a number cube: 1, 2, 2, 3, 3, 3. What is the probability that 2 lands up when the cube is tossed?

Sales Tax

(pages 72–73)

Solve each problem. Read the questions carefully! Sometimes, you will need to find the amount of sales tax. Other times, you will need to find the total cost.

_____   1. The price of a bracelet is $24.95. The sales tax is 6%. Find the amount of tax.

_____   2. The price of a lamp is $54.75. The sales tax is 5%. Find the amount of tax.

_____   3. The price of a suitcase is $180. The sales tax is $7\frac{1}{2}$%. Find the amount of tax.

_____   4. The price of a camera is $154. A lens kit is $49. The sales tax is 7%. You buy the camera and lens kit. Find the amount of tax you pay.

_____   5. The price of a pair of socks is $1.99. The sales tax is 4%. You buy 6 pairs of socks. Find the amount of tax you pay.

_____   6. The price of a guitar is $69.99. The sales tax is 5%. Find the total cost.

_____   7. The price of a sewing machine is $189.50. The sales tax is 6%. Find the total cost.

_____   8. The price of a sleeping bag is $49.99. The sales tax is $6\frac{1}{2}$%. Find the total cost.

_____   9. The price of a table-tennis table is $139.98. A set of paddles, balls, and net is $23.99. The sales tax is 7%. Find the total cost.

_____   10. The price of a black-and-white TV is $79.99. A color TV is $159.99. The sales tax is 5%. How much more would you pay for the color TV than for the black-and-white TV?

_____   11. The price of a can of tennis balls is $2.49. The sales tax is 6%. Find the total cost of 4 cans of tennis balls.

_____   12. The price of a table is $150. Chairs are $35 each. The sales tax is 7%. Find the total cost of a table and 4 chairs.

Discounts
(pages 74–75)

Solve each problem. Read the question carefully.

_____ 1. A 3-speed bike originally sold for $115.99. This week the store is giving a 15% discount off the original price. What is the discount?

_____ 2. Roller skates usually sell for $49.99. The store is having a 25% close-out sale. How much will the discount be during the close-out sale?

_____ 3. Clock radios usually sell for $19.99 each. They are on sale for 20% off the original price. Find the sale price of a radio.

_____ 4. A home computer sells for $299.99. A color monitor sells for $249.99. A 15% discount is given to people who buy both the computer and the monitor. How much is the computer and monitor?

_____ 5. A manual typewriter usually sells for $76.99. An electric typewriter usually sells for $194.99. A 20% discount is given on each typewriter this week. How much more does the electric typewriter cost than the manual typewriter this week?

_____ 6. Warm-up suits are on sale for $10 off the original price of $50. What is the percent of discount? (Hint: Look at Example B on page 74.)

_____ 7. Boots are on sale for $12.50 off the original price of $50. What is the percent of discount?

_____ 8. During a 15%-off sale, the discount on a camera was $30. What was the original price of the camera?

_____ 9. A telescope is on sale for $75. The original price was $125. What is the percent of discount? (Hint: First find the amount of discount.)

_____ 10. A microscope is on sale for $39.99. The original price was $49.99. What is the percent of discount?

Time Cards

(pages 76–77)

Answer the questions. Use the time card on page 76 for Problems 1–4.

1. Next month, Clay will get a raise. He will earn $5.90 per hour. He will receive time and a half for overtime. How much will Clay be paid per hour of overtime?

2. The week after his raise, Clay worked the same number of hours he worked during the week ending April 30. He was paid time and a half for the time over 40 hours he worked. How much did he earn during the first week after his raise?

3. One week after his raise, Clay worked 36 hours. The next week he worked 39 hours. How much more did he earn during the week he worked 39 hours?

4. The following week Clay worked 43 hours. How much more did he earn the week he worked 43 hours than the week he worked 39 hours?

Use the following time card to answer Problems 5–8.

	IN	OUT		IN	OUT	HOURS WORKED
Mon.	9:00	12:00	L	1:00	5:00	
Tues.	9:00	1:30	U	2:00	5:30	
Wed.	10:00	2:00	N	2:30	6:00	
Thurs.	9:00	12:30	C	1:30	7:00	
Fri.	9:00	2:00	H			
Sat.				12:00	6:00	
					Total Hours	

Party Shop

Name _Jean Brown_

Week Ending _July 31_

5. Complete the "HOURS WORKED" column on the time card for Jean Brown.

6. Jean is paid $7.20 an hour. How much did Jean earn on Wednesday?

7. Jean is paid time and a half for the time over 40 hours that she works. How much is she paid per hour of overtime?

8. How much did Jean earn during the week ending July 31?

9. Vern earns $8.50 per hour. She earns time and a half if she works more than 35 hours a week. Vern worked 38 hours last week. How much did she earn?

10. This week Vern earned $289. How many hours did she work?

114

Sampling

(pages 78–79)

Answer these questions. Use the sample chart on page 78 for Problems 1–3.

_____ 1. What percent of students in the sample like jazz music best?

_____ 2. There are 890 students in the school. Based on the sample, how many students in the school like jazz music best?

_____ 3. What percent of the students in the sample like country *or* jazz music best?

There are 1,250 students at Murphy School. The school newspaper reporter asked 50 students to name their favorite type of fiction. The results are shown in the chart.

```
┌─────────────────────────────────────┐
│          Murphy School              │
│                                     │
│      Favorite Type of Fiction       │
│  Adventure      ####  ####  //   12 │
│  Mystery        ####  ####       10 │
│  Historical Novel  ####  ///      8 │
│  Romance        ####  //          7 │
│  Horror         ####               5 │
│  Science Fiction  ####  ///        8 │
└─────────────────────────────────────┘
```

_____ 4. What percent of students in the sample like mystery stories best?

_____ 5. Based on this sample, how many students in the school like mystery stories best?

_____ 6. What percent of students in the sample like adventure stories *or* science fiction best?

_____ 7. Based on this sample, how many students in the school like adventure stories *or* science fiction best?

_____ 8. Based on this sample, how many more students in the school like romance than horror stories?

_____ 9. There was a random sample of 50 customers at a grocery store. Twenty said they ate fish at least once a week. Based on this sample, how many of the 4,500 customers who shopped that day eat fish at least once a week?

_____ 10. There was a random sample of 100 radio listeners. Thirty people said they would rather listen to talk shows than to music. Now suppose 1,000 radio listeners are sampled. Based on the earlier sample, how many will rather listen to talk shows than to music?

Whole-Book Review

Read and reread each word problem. Then follow the directions to show your solution to the problem.

1. Sports World is having a one-day sale on skateboards. All skateboards are on sale for 30% off the original price. During the sale, Phil bought a skateboard that originally sold for $49. What was the sale price of the skateboard?
   a. Underline the question.
   b. Circle the needed facts in the problem.

   c. Describe your plan: _____
   _____

   d. If an estimate can be made, show it here: _____

   e. Carry out your plan. Answer: _____

   f. Check your answer. If you got an incorrect answer, tell how you know it is wrong. Then write the correct answer.

   _____
   _____

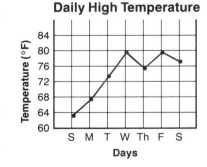

2. How many degrees warmer was the high temperature on Wednesday than the high temperature on Sunday?
   a. Underline the question.
   b. Circle the needed facts in the problem.

   c. Describe your plan: _____
   _____

   d. If an estimate can be made, show it here: _____

   e. Carry out your plan. Answer: _____

   f. Check your answer. If you got an incorrect answer, tell how you know it is wrong. Then write the correct answer.

   _____
   _____

3. Pat bought 16 yards of fabric to re-cover her sofa. This is $9\frac{1}{2}$ yards more than she bought to re-cover her chair. How much fabric did Pat buy to re-cover her chair?

   a. Underline the question.
   b. Circle the needed facts in the problem.

   c. Describe your plan: _____

   _____

   d. If an estimate can be made, show it here: _____

   e. Carry out your plan. Answer: _____

   f. Check your answer. If you got an incorrect answer, tell how you know it is wrong. Then write the correct answer.

   _____

   _____

4. Anne had $389.15 in her checking account. She wrote a check to Mort's Market for $23.10. How much money does Anne have left in her checking account?

   a. Underline the question.
   b. Circle the needed facts in the problem.

   c. Describe your plan: _____

   _____

   d. If an estimate can be made, show it here: _____

   e. Carry out your plan. Answer: _____

   f. Check your answer. If you got an incorrect answer, tell how you know it is wrong. Then write the correct answer.

   _____

   _____

5. Ruth can type 3 pages in 20 minutes. How many pages can Ruth type in 1 hour?
   a. Underline the question.
   b. Circle the needed facts in the problem.

   c. Describe your plan: _____

   _____

   d. If an estimate can be made, show it here: _____

   e. Carry out your plan. Answer: _____

   f. Check your answer. If you got an incorrect answer, tell how you know it is wrong. Then write the correct answer.

   _____

   _____

Snyders' Budget

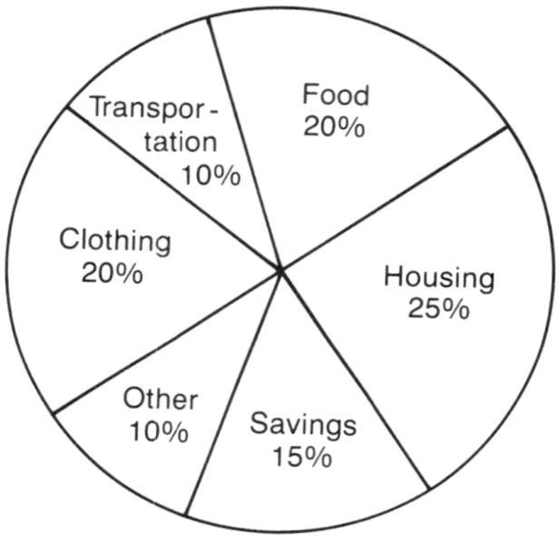

6. The graph shows how the Snyders plan to budget their money. Their take-home pay last month totaled $1,800. How much should they have put away for savings?
   a. Underline the question.
   b. Circle the needed facts in the problem.

   c. Describe your plan: _____

   _____

   d. If an estimate can be made, show it here: _____

   e. Carry out your plan. Answer: _____

   f. Check your answer. If you got an incorrect answer, tell how you know it is wrong. Then write the correct answer.

   _____

   _____

7. Gary bought a pair of boots and 3 pairs of socks for $41. The boots cost $35. How much did *each* pair of socks cost?
   a. Underline the question.
   b. Circle the needed facts in the problem.

   c. Describe your plan: _____

   _____

   d. If an estimate can be made, show it here: _____

   e. Carry out your plan. Answer: _____
   f. Check your answer. If you got an incorrect answer, tell how you know it is wrong. Then write the correct answer.

   _____

   _____

8. Fran invested $5,000 at 6% simple interest for $2\frac{1}{2}$ years. How much interest did she earn?
   a. Underline the question.
   b. Circle the needed facts in the problem.

   c. Describe your plan: _____

   _____

   d. If an estimate can be made, show it here: _____

   e. Carry out your plan. Answer: _____
   f. Check your answer. If you got an incorrect answer, tell how you know it is wrong. Then write the correct answer.

   _____

   _____

This is the end of the Whole-Book Review.

Appendix

Metric System   ## Customary System

Length

10 millimeters (mm)	= 1 centimeter (cm)	12 inches (in.)	= 1 foot (ft.)
10 centimeters / 100 millimeters	= 1 decimeter (dm)	3 feet / 36 inches	= 1 yard (yd.)
10 decimeters / 100 centimeters	= 1 meter (m)	1,760 yards / 5,280 feet	= 1 mile (mi.)
1,000 meters	= 1 kilometer (km)	6,076 feet	= 1 nautical mile

Area

100 square millimeters (mm^2)	= 1 square centimeter (cm^2)	144 square inches (sq. in.)	= 1 square foot (sq. ft.)
10,000 square centimeters	= 1 square meter (m^2)	9 square feet	= 1 square yard (sq. yd.)
100 square meters	= 1 are (a)	4,840 square yards	= 1 acre (A.)
10,000 square meters	= 1 hectare (ha)	640 acres	= 1 square mile (sq. mi.)

Volume

1,000 cubic millimeters (mm^3)	= 1 cubic centimeter (cm^3)	1,728 cubic inches (cu. in.)	= 1 cubic foot (cu. ft.)
1,000 cubic centimeters	= 1 cubic decimeter (dm^3)	27 cubic feet	= 1 cubic yard (cu. yd.)
1,000,000 cubic centimeters	= 1 cubic meter (m^3)		

Mass/Weight

1,000 milligrams (mg)	= 1 gram (g)	16 ounces (oz.)	= 1 pound (lb.)
1,000 grams	= 1 kilogram (kg)	2,000 pounds	= 1 ton (T.)
1,000 kilograms	= 1 metric ton (t)		

Capacity

1,000 milliliters (mL)	= 1 liter (L)	8 fluid ounces (fl. oz.)	= 1 cup (c.)
		2 cups	= 1 pint (pt.)
		2 pints	= 1 quart (qt.)
		4 quarts	= 1 gallon (gal.)

Time

60 seconds = 1 minute	365 days	
60 minutes = 1 hour	52 weeks	= 1 year
24 hours = 1 day	12 months	
7 days = 1 week	366 days	= 1 leap year

Operations Chart

Action	Operation
Joining different-sized groups (a different number in each group) to find a total	Addition
Separating Objects to find a group that is left or **Comparing two groups** to find the difference	Subtraction
Joining equal groups to find a total	Multiplication
Sharing equally to find the size of each group or **Making groups of a given size** to find the number of groups	Division

Geometric Formulas

Perimeter (P)
(the distance around a figure)

square	$P = 4s$
rectangle	$P = 2l + 2w$

Circumference (C)
(the distance around a circle)

circle	$C = \pi d$
or	$C = 2\pi r$

Area (A)
(the number of square units enclosed by a figure)

square	$A = s^2$
rectangle	$A = lw$
parallelogram	$A = bh$
triangle	$A = \frac{1}{2}bh$
circle	$A = \pi r^2$

Note: $\pi = \frac{22}{7}$ or 3.14

Volume (V)
(the number of cubic units enclosed by a three-dimensional shape)

rectangular prism

$V = lwh$

square

s (side)

rectangle

w (width)

l (length)

triangle

h (height)

b (base)

parallelogram

h (height)

b (base)

circle

d (diameter)

r (radius)

rectangular prism

h (height)

w (width)

l (length)

Other Formulas

distance = rate × time, or $d = rt$

interest = principal × rate × time, or $i = prt$

unit price = $\dfrac{\text{total cost}}{\text{number of units}}$

probability = $\dfrac{\text{number of favorable outcomes}}{\text{number of possible outcomes}}$

sales tax = rate of sales tax × price of item

total cost = price + sales tax

discount = rate of discount × original price

sale price = original price − discount

total pay = regular pay + overtime pay